Title: "Unleashing Potential: The Power and Benefits of Embedded Remote Teams"

Table of Contents

INTRODUCTION

Welcome to ''Unleashing Potential: The Power and Benefits of Embedded Remote Teams.'' In this dynamic era of work, the traditional boundaries of office spaces are expanding, and organizations are tapping into the transformative potential of embedded remote teams. This e-book explores the profound advantages, strategies, and innovations that come with embracing remote work as a strategic element of organizational success.

As we delve into the chapters that follow, we'll navigate the evolution of remote work, examine the advantages that embedded remote teams bring to the table, and provide practical insights into building a foundation that fosters collaboration and productivity. From overcoming challenges to showcasing success stories and delving into the future of work, this e-book is your guide to navigating the changing landscape of the modern workplace.

In this time of phenomenal network and mechanical headway, the conventional ideas of working environment elements are going through a significant change. "Releasing Potential: The Power and Advantages of Installed Remote Groups" dives into this change in outlook, where the limits of office spaces break down, leading to a unique scene of cooperative prospects. As associations explore the developing idea of work, we investigate the undiscovered supply of expected inside implanted remote groups, imagining a future where development, efficiency, and adaptability join to rethink the manner in which we work. Go along with us in this investigation of another wilderness where groups break liberated from regular requirements, opening their maximum capacity in the domain of far-off joint effort.

Join us on this journey as we uncover the keys to unleashing the true potential of embedded remote teams and shaping the future of work for organizations and individuals alike.

Definition of Embedded Remote Team

An Embedded remote Team is a strong gathering of experts circulated across various areas yet unpredictably woven into the texture of an association's tasks. These groups consistently incorporate with the more extensive organization structure, teaming up basically while keeping areas of strength for the hierarchical objectives and culture. This approach goes past the customary remote work arrangement, as individuals become fundamental parts of explicit ventures or divisions, breaking down geological hindrances to accomplish a bound together and productive work process. The implanted remote group model cultivates adaptability, advancement, and cross-useful cooperation in the developing scene of present-day work.

Evolution of Remote work

The revolution of remote work has been a unique excursion formed by mechanical progressions, changing mentalities towards work, and worldwide occasions. At first, remote work was, to a great extent, restricted by innovative requirements. In any case, with the ascent of the web, specialized devices, and cooperative stages, the scene changed.

The mid-2000s saw the development of working from home, permitting people to telecommute. This idea picked up speed throughout the long term; however, it was the 2020 Corona virus pandemic that went about as an impetus, moving remote work into the standard. Constrained variations during lockdowns displayed the possibility and advantages of remote work, setting off a change in outlook on how organizations see and execute adaptable work game plans.

Organizations began embracing mixture models, mixing remote and in-office work. This development isn't simply innovative but additionally social, testing conventional ideas of a concentrated work environment. The continuous development of remote work mirrors a more extensive cultural shift towards adaptability, underlining results over actual presence and encouraging a more comprehensive and versatile way to deal with work.

Moreover, the development of remote work has prompted a reexamination of efficiency measurements. As associations progressively focus on results over hours spent at an actual office, the center has moved to estimate expectations and accomplishments. This shift has engaged people to structure their work in manners that suit their ways of life, adding to a better balance between serious and fun activities.

The advanced traveler culture has additionally arisen, permitting experts to work from any place around the world. This pattern has been worked with by the pervasiveness of the fast web and a developing affirmation that efficiency can flourish past customary office limits. The development of remote work is probably going to include progressing refinements in distant joint effort apparatuses, the foundation of clear remote work strategies, and a constant transformation to the changing requirements and assumptions for the labor force. This extraordinary excursion addresses a change in where work occurs as well as a crucial reshaping of how we conceptualize and move toward work in the cutting edge time.

Furthermore, the advancement of remote work is affecting authoritative designs. Conventional ordered progressions are giving way to additional adaptable, decentralized models that oblige distant cooperation. This shift is driven by the acknowledgment that powerful correspondence, shared objectives, and a solid organizational culture can flourish in virtual conditions. The rising accentuation on representative prosperity and psychological well-being is one more outstanding part of this advancement. Remote work has incited a reassessment of business-related stressors and the significance of establishing steady conditions. Organizations are embracing arrangements that focus on emotional wellness, recognizing the difficulties and advantages related to remote work. As far as innovation, manufactured reasoning, and mechanization are probably going to assume a more critical part in working with remote errands and improving virtual coordinated effort. As development keeps, finding some kind of harmony between utilizing innovation for effectiveness and keeping up with the human association will be a key thought.

Generally, the development of remote work stretches out past a simple change in the area; it's a multi-layered change impacting society, hierarchical elements, innovation use, and the general prosperity of the labor force. The evolution of remote work is reshaping talent acquisition and retention strategies. Companies are broadening their geographical scope when recruiting tapping into a global talent pool. This approach enhances diversity and enables organizations to access specialized skills that might not be locally available. The concept of 'work from anywhere' is gaining traction, allowing employees the freedom to choose their preferred location for work. This evolution demands a reevaluation of traditional employment contracts and the development of policies that accommodate diverse work settings.

Importantly, the evolution of remote work is influencing urban planning and real estate. The reduced reliance on centralized offices has implications for city infrastructures and may lead to the development of more flexible and communal workspaces. As remote work continues to evolve, it underscores the need for agility and adaptability in both individuals and organizations. Embracing this shift involves navigating a complex interplay of technology, culture, policies, and individual preferences to create a future where remote work is not just a response to external circumstances but an intentional and strategic choice.

Purpose and scope of this EBook

Purpose:

The purpose of this e-book is to empower readers with a comprehensive understanding of "Unleashing Potential: The Power and Benefits of Embedded Remote Teams." It aims to shed light on the transformative nature of embedded remote teams, emphasizing the untapped capabilities within this model. The e-book aspires to be a guide, offering insights into the dynamics, advantages, and strategic considerations involved in fostering embedded remote teams. Whether you're a business leader, team manager, or an individual contributor, the e-book seeks to provide actionable knowledge to navigate and harness the potential of this evolving paradigm in the modern workplace.

This e-book is also designed to be a catalyst for change, inspiring individuals and organizations to rethink their approach to work in the context of embedded remote teams. It aims to instill a sense of curiosity and exploration, encouraging readers to embrace the potential within this evolving paradigm. Whether you're seeking ways to optimize team collaboration, adapt to the changing landscape of work, or unlock new possibilities for your organization, this e-book serves as a guide for empowerment and transformation.

Another purpose of this digital book is to be a provocative asset that goes past the outer layer of installed remote groups. It looks to rouse an outlook shift, testing previously established inclinations about customary work structures and empowering a reconsideration of how groups team up. By offering a mix of hypothetical bits of knowledge and viable direction, the digital book furnishes peruses with the information and inspiration to tackle the maximum capacity of implanted remote groups. Whether you are a business chief, HR proficient, or a singular giver, the inspiration is to encourage a more profound comprehension of this developing work worldview and its extraordinary effect on the expert scene.

**Scope:

The extent of the digital book is sweeping, covering the range of points applicable to implanted remote groups. From the verifiable setting and innovative underpinnings to the nuanced parts of group elements, correspondence techniques, and the future direction of remote work, it gives a far-reaching investigation. Contextual investigations, interviews with industry specialists, and significant experiences will be coordinated to make a balanced point of view. Moreover, the degree reaches out to tending to possible difficulties, guaranteeing that the digital book fills in as a reasonable aide for exploring the intricacies of executing and flourishing inside implanted remote groups. Generally, the degree plans to convey a comprehensive and important asset for people and associations exploring the developing scene of work.

The scope of this e-book encompasses a deep dive into various facets of embedded remote teams. It will explore topics such as the historical context of remote work, the technological advancements shaping its evolution, and the cultural shifts influencing its adoption. Practical aspects, including strategies for effective collaboration, tools for remote teamwork, and case studies illustrating successful implementations, will be covered. The e-book will address the advantages, acknowledge potential challenges, and provide insights on mitigating them. By keeping theory and real-world application in check, the scope ensures that readers gain a holistic understanding of embedded remote teams, enabling them to leverage this approach for enhanced productivity and innovation. The scope of the e-book extends beyond a mere overview, delving into the intricacies of embedded remote teams. It will cover key themes such as the psychological aspects of remote work, strategies for building a robust culture of teamwork in a remote setting, and the role of leadership in fostering success. Practical insights, real-world examples, and expert perspectives will be woven together to provide a rich tapestry of knowledge. Additionally, the e-book will explore emerging trends, potential future developments, and the long-term implications of embracing embedded remote teams. By addressing both the present and the future, the scope ensures that readers gain a forward-thinking perspective on the transformative power of this innovative work model. The extent of the digital book is sweeping, covering the range of points applicable to implanted remote groups. From the verifiable setting and innovative underpinnings to the nuanced parts of group elements, correspondence techniques, and the future direction of remote work, it gives a far-reaching investigation.

Contextual investigations, interviews with industry specialists, and significant experiences will be coordinated to make a balanced perspective. Moreover, the degree reaches out to tending to possible difficulties, guaranteeing that the digital book fills in as a reasonable aide for exploring the intricacies of executing and flourishing inside implanted remote groups. Generally, the degree plans to convey a comprehensive and important asset for people and associations exploring the developing scene of work.

The Advantages of Embedded Remote Teams

In the modern landscape of work, embedded remote teams offer a myriad of advantages that extend beyond the traditional office setting. This chapter explores these benefits, emphasizing the transformative impact they can have on both organizations and their employees.

Flexibility and Work-Life Balance

Embedded remote teams empower employees to create a work environment that suits their individual needs. This flexibility fosters a healthier work-life balance, leading to increased job satisfaction and overall well-being.

Access to Global Talent

By embracing remote work, organizations can reach out to a wide range of international talent. It not only broadens the skill set within the team but also brings in fresh perspectives and innovative ideas.

•Increased Productivity and Efficiency:

Remote work often leads to heightened productivity, as employees can tailor their work environment to maximize focus. The elimination of commute time and reduction in workplace distractions contribute to more efficient work processes.

Cost Savings for Organizations:

Adopting embedded remote teams can result in significant cost savings for organizations. Reduced overhead costs, such as office space and utilities, contribute to a more streamlined budget.

Enhanced Employee Retention:

Offering remote work options, as seen in embedded remote teams, can be a powerful retention strategy. Employees often value the flexibility provided by remote labor, resulting in a better level of job satisfaction and a greater likelihood of staying with the organization in the long term.

Reduced Commuting Stress:

By eliminating the need for daily commutes, embedded remote teams contribute to a reduction in commuting-related stress for team members. It saves time and positively impacts mental well-being, contributing to a more engaged and focused workforce.

Diverse Perspectives and Inclusion:

The global nature of embedded remote teams fosters diversity and inclusion. Team members from various backgrounds and cultures bring unique perspectives, enriching the team's problem-solving capabilities and promoting a more inclusive workplace culture.

Agile Response to Challenges:

Embedded remote teams are inherently equipped to respond agilely to unforeseen challenges, such as sudden disruptions or crises. The distributed nature of the team allows for quick adaptation, ensuring business continuity in dynamic and uncertain circumstances.

Environmental Impact:

With fewer employees commuting to a centralized location, embedded remote teams contribute to a reduction in the carbon footprint associated with daily commuting. This aligns with sustainability goals and reflects a commitment to environmentally conscious practices.

Improved Workforce Continuity:

Distributed teams enhance workforce continuity by mitigating risks associated with single points of failure. In the case of disturbances, whether natural catastrophes or public health emergencies, the distributed nature of the team ensures that work can continue seamlessly.

Customized Work Environments:

Embedded remote teams allow individuals to create personalized workspaces tailored to their preferences. This customization contributes to increased comfort and motivation, enhancing overall job satisfaction and performance.

Time Zone Diversity for 24/7 Operations:

The geographical dispersion of embedded remote teams enables organizations to leverage time zone differences strategically. It can result in extended working hours or even 24/7 operations, facilitating continuous progress on projects and improved responsiveness to global clients.

Wider Talent Retention:

Being able to operate remotely gives organizations the option to retain valuable talent that might otherwise consider leaving due to geographical constraints. Higher staff retention rates may result from it, especially for individuals who value the opportunity to work from their preferred locations.

Autonomous Decision-Making:

Embedded remote teams often empower individual team members to make more autonomous decisions. It speeds up decision-making processes and instills a sense of ownership and accountability among team members.

Reduced Office Politics:

The virtual nature of embedded remote teams can contribute to a reduction in traditional office politics. Physical distance minimizes the likelihood of power struggles or unnecessary conflicts, allowing teams to focus more on collaboration and achieving shared goals.

Increased Employee Satisfaction:

The flexibility, autonomy, and diverse work environments offered by embedded remote teams contribute to higher levels of employee satisfaction. Satisfied employees are generally more engaged and motivated, and probably going to have a good effect on the team's performance as a whole.

Adaptability to Individual Work Styles:

Embedded remote teams accommodate various work styles, recognizing that individuals may have different peak productivity times or preferred methods of approaching tasks. This adaptability fosters an environment where each team member can optimize their contributions.

Broader Learning Opportunities:

Virtual collaboration within embedded remote teams exposes team members to a wide range of digital tools and communication platforms. This constant exposure encourages continuous learning and adaptation to evolving technologies, contributing to the professional development of team members.

As we delve into the intricate details of each of these advantages, it becomes evident that embedded remote teams represent more than just a reaction to the evolving landscape of work; they embody a strategic shift toward unlocking unparalleled potential for both organizations and their workforce. The flexibility and work-life balance offered by embedded remote teams transcend the conventional constraints of a physical office, providing individuals with the freedom to structure their work in alignment with personal lifestyles. This autonomy is not merely a response to changing times but a strategic move to enhance employee satisfaction, well-being, and, ultimately, productivity. Access to global talent is not merely a consequence of technological advancements; it is a deliberate strategy to assemble teams with diverse skills and perspectives. By transcending geographical boundaries, organizations strategically position themselves to thrive in a competitive global market, leveraging the unique strengths each team member brings. Increased productivity and efficiency in embedded remote teams are not accidental outcomes; they are the result of a deliberate restructuring of work dynamics. Empowering individuals to work in environments conducive to their focus and creativity is a strategic choice that aligns with organizational goals of heightened performance and adaptability. The cost savings associated with embedded remote teams extend beyond mere financial considerations. It is a strategic decision to allocate resources more efficiently, redirecting funds toward innovation, employee development, or other strategic initiatives that propel the organization forward. As we dissect these advantages, it becomes apparent that embedded remote teams are a conscious and forward-thinking strategy. This strategic shift acknowledges the evolving nature of work and positions organizations to unlock unprecedented potential, fostering a work environment where both individuals and the organization thrive in tandem.

Building a Strong Foundation

- Laying out Clear Correspondence Channels: Building a powerful establishment starts with the foundation of clear correspondence channels. It includes choosing proper specialized apparatuses as well as characterizing correspondence conventions. Groups should express assumptions for reaction times, favored channels for various sorts of correspondence, and rules for virtual gatherings. By encouraging straightforward and effective correspondence, groups can connect the actual distance and develop a mutual perspective among individuals.

- Utilizing Innovation for Collaboration: The groundwork of implanted remote groups depends vigorously on utilizing innovation for consistent cooperation. It includes the essential choice and execution of joint effort devices, project the executives' stages and correspondence programming. Successful utilization of innovation guarantees that colleagues can team up continuously, share assets easily, and keep a firm work process. The essential mix of innovation lines up with the general objective of improving proficiency and efficiency in a virtual workplace.

- Encouraging a Remote-Accommodating Culture: Developing a remote-accommodating society is central to building areas of strength implanted in remote groups. It includes laying out standards and practices that perceive and oblige the special parts of remote work. Group pioneers assume a critical part in establishing the vibe for a culture that values results over simple presence. Empowering open correspondence, perceiving accomplishments, and making virtual spaces for casual collaborations add to a feeling of having a place and group union. A remote-accommodating society isn't just about adjusting to change but effectively embracing and praising the advantages of a conveyed labor force.

In rundown, constructing serious areas of strength implanted in remote groups is a purposeful cycle that includes laying out successful correspondence channels, utilizing innovation decisively, and encouraging a culture that embraces the subtleties of remote work. Every component adds to the versatility and progress of implanted remote groups, situating them to flourish in the steadily developing scene of current work.

Proactive Group Alignment: Guarantee major areas of strength by proactively adjusting colleagues to the association's objectives and values. Routinely convey the more extensive vision, mission, and goals, underscoring how each colleague adds to the aggregate achievement. This arrangement encourages a common feeling of direction and responsibility, pivotal for remote groups that might not have the day-to-day actual presence to support a hierarchical character.

- Laying out Clear Expectations: Lucidity is key while working in implanted remote groups. Obviously, characterize jobs, obligations, and assumptions for each colleague. It mitigates possible false impressions and engages people to take responsibility for assignments. Laying out clear assumptions sets the foundation for responsibility and guarantees that everybody grasps their commitment to the group's general achievement.

- Persistent Learning and Development: Building areas of strength for a pledge to the ceaseless learning and improvement of colleagues. Work with open doors for expertise improvement, give admittance to important assets, and support a culture of information sharing. it lifts individual development as well as adds to the group's aggregate skill, making it more versatile and strong despite advancing difficulties.

- Focusing on Prosperity and Mental Health: A powerful establishment remembers a concentration on the prosperity and psychological well-being of colleagues. Remote work can, at times, obscure the limits of individual and expert life. Energize ordinary breaks, layout arrangements that advance balance between fun and serious activities, and give assets to psychological wellness support. Focusing on prosperity establishes a positive and strong workplace, which is vital for supported group execution.

- Dexterous Dynamic Processes: Implant dexterity into dynamic cycles. In a remote setting, fast and informed choices are fundamental. Lay out smoothed dynamic structures, influence cooperative instruments for input, and enable colleagues to add to the dynamic cycle. This readiness guarantees that the group can adjust quickly to changing conditions and immediately take advantage of rising chances.

By consolidating these components, associations can build an establishment that not only backs the prompt requirements of implanted remote groups but also positions them for long–haul achievement and versatility in the unique scene of present-day work.

Overcoming Challenges

Overcoming Challenges in Embedded Remote Teams:

- **Addressing Communication Barriers:** Effectively overcoming communication barriers is crucial for the success of embedded remote teams. This involves employing a multi-faceted approach, including the use of diverse communication tools, scheduling regular check-ins, and establishing clear communication protocols. Emphasis should be placed on promoting open and transparent communication encouraging team members to express themselves freely. Additionally, providing training on virtual communication etiquette can enhance the effectiveness of remote interactions, ensuring that information flows seamlessly despite physical distances.

- **Managing Time Zone Differences:** Time zone variations can present a significant challenge in embedded remote teams. Mitigating this challenge requires a strategic approach, such as implementing flexible work hours or adopting a "follow-the-sun" work model for global teams. Clear guidelines on when synchronous communication is essential and when asynchronous methods are acceptable help in managing expectations. Leveraging time zone overlaps for crucial meetings or collaborative sessions can also foster efficient communication and collaboration.

- **Nurturing Team Cohesion and Collaboration:** Building a strong sense of cohesion and collaboration within an embedded remote team demands intentional efforts. It includes organizing virtual team-building activities, establishing chances for informal contacts, and cultivating a feeling of common purpose. Video conferences, collaborative platforms, and social channels can serve as mediums for team bonding. Leaders play a pivotal role in nurturing a collaborative culture by recognizing individual contributions, promoting teamwork, and establishing channels for feedback. Regular team meetings that go beyond task-related discussions to include social elements contribute to a more cohesive and connected team.

Ensuring Inclusivity: Feeling alone can occasionally result from working remotely. We'll examine ways to ensure inclusivity, including involving all team members in decision-making processes and creating opportunities for virtual interactions.

- **Building Trust through Transparency:** Straightforwardness is vital to beating difficulties in remote groups. Energize open sharing of data, project updates, and difficulties looked at by colleagues. This forms trust inside the group, as everybody is in total agreement regarding advance and expected deterrents. Straightforward correspondence encourages a cooperative environment where people feel educated and upheld.

- **Strong on boarding Processes:** Viable on boarding is fundamental, particularly for new individuals joining remote groups. Give exhaustive on boarding materials, lead virtual direction meetings, and match newbie with experienced colleagues for mentorship. A solid on boarding process guarantees that colleagues are outfitted with the information and assets they need, lessening the probability of false impressions and upgrading the generally crew union.

- **Stressing Results over Activity:** Shift the concentration from estimating hours attempted to assessing results accomplished. This approach checks potential difficulties connected with observing individual work in a remote setting. At the point when the accentuation is on results, colleagues are enabled to deal with their time productively and contribute genuinely, cultivating a culture of responsibility and trust.

- **Carrying out Normal Registrations and Criticism Loops:** Laying out normal registrations and criticism circles is imperative for tending to difficulties quickly. Customary one-on-one gatherings, group registrations, and input meetings give potential chances to discuss worries, celebrate victories, and distinguish regions for development. This continuous exchange guarantees that issues are distinguished early, considering ideal intercession and goal.

- **Empowering Information Sharing:** Combating the storehouse impact in remote groups includes effectively reassuring information sharing. Carry out stages and practices that work with the trading of data, best practices, and examples learned. This aggregate information sharing adds to a more educated and versatile group, separating boundaries that might emerge from data storage or disconnection.

- **Laying out Clear Conventions for Struggle Resolution:** Remote work can, in some cases, enhance errors. Laying out clear conventions for compromise is time-sensitive. Characterize channels for tending to clash, support open conversations, and give assets to intercession when essential. Having an organized way to deal with compromise keeps issues from heightening and advances a solid group dynamic.

- **Putting resources into Proficient Improvement Opportunities:** Remote groups benefit from nonstop mastering and expertise advancement. Putting resources into proficient advancement potential opens doors that take care of the particular requirements of remote colleagues. It can incorporate virtual instructional meetings, studios on distant coordinated effort apparatuses, and courses that upgrade remote work abilities. An exceptional and persistently developing group is more ready to handle difficulties that emerge in a unique workplace.

- **Adjusting Independence and Collaboration:** Finding the right harmony between independence and joint effort is fundamental. While remote work underscores individual obligation, encouraging cooperation stays essential. Lay out clear assumptions about when cooperative endeavors are required and give stages that work with simple correspondence. This equilibrium guarantees that colleagues have the independence to succeed in their jobs while contributing successfully to group goals.

- **Checking and Moderating Distant Burnout:** It can prompt burnout. Execute systems to screen and relieve remote burnout, like empowering breaks, setting sensible assumptions for working hours, and advancing a culture that values prosperity. Customary registrations on responsibility and feelings of anxiety add to a strong climate that focuses on the psychological and profound well-being of colleagues.

- **Adjusting to Developing Technologies:** The fast advancement of innovation requires consistent variation. Guarantee that your remote group keeps up to date with new devices and stages that improve coordinated effort and efficiency. Consistently survey the innovative necessities of the group and give preparing on arising innovations, empowering colleagues to actually use the most recent headway.

Consolidating these extra methodologies upgrades the strength and flexibility of implanted remote groups, situating them to really defeat difficulties and flourish in a unique workplace.

Showcasing Success Stories:

Showcasing success stories in the context of companies embracing embedded remote teams involves highlighting real-world examples and experiences to illustrate the positive outcomes of such a working model.

Case Studies of Companies Embracing Embedded Remote Teams:
Share detailed case studies of companies that have successfully
implemented embedded remote teams. Discuss the challenges they
faced, the solutions they implemented, and the tangible benefits
they reaped. Provide insights into industries, team sizes, and
specific roles that thrived in this remote setup.

Lessons Learned: Summarize key lessons that companies have
learned through their experiences with embedded remote teams.
This could include insights into effective communication
strategies, tools that proved essential, and adjustments made to
workflow and processes to optimize remote collaboration.

Best Practices: Offer a set of best practices derived from successful
cases. This might include tips on fostering team cohesion,
maintaining productivity, leveraging technology for effective
communication, and creating a supportive virtual work culture.
You can use these best practices as a reference for other companies
considering or currently transitioning to embedded remote teams.

Employee Testimonials: Incorporate personal stories and
testimonials from employees within these companies who have
experienced the transition to embedded remote teams. Highlight

their perspectives on the positive aspects, challenges overcome, and how the remote setup has impacted their work-life balance and job satisfaction.

Measurable Outcomes: Quantify the success by presenting measurable outcomes such as increased productivity, cost savings, improved employee satisfaction scores, or any other relevant metrics. Concrete data adds credibility and provides a clear picture of the tangible benefits achieved through the adoption of embedded remote teams.

Adaptability and Innovation: Illustrate how companies have demonstrated adaptability and innovation in the face of change. Showcase instances where remote teams have been instrumental in driving new ideas, projects, or strategies, emphasizing the positive impact on the company's overall growth and competitiveness.

Scalability and Global Reach: Explore how embedded remote teams have allowed companies to scale operations more efficiently and tap into a global talent pool. Discuss examples where companies expanded their reach, accessing diverse skill sets and perspectives from different geographical locations.

Sustainability and Environmental Impact: Consider including information on how embracing embedded remote teams aligns with sustainability goals. Discuss reduced commuting, lower office energy consumption, and the positive environmental impact of a distributed workforce.

Inclusive Work Culture: Highlight how embedded remote teams contribute to building a more inclusive work culture. Showcase examples of companies fostering diversity and inclusion by providing equal opportunities to talent regardless of geographical location, thus promoting a more diverse workforce.

Agile Project Management: Demonstrate how companies have embraced agile project management methodologies within embedded remote teams. Discuss how this flexibility and adaptability have allowed them can keep ahead of the competition, innovate swiftly, and react quickly to shifting market conditions.

Cost-Efficiency and Savings: Explore how companies have realized cost efficiencies by reducing overhead expenses associated with maintaining a physical office space. Discuss savings in terms of real estate, utilities, and other operational costs, providing a financial perspective on the benefits of remote work.

Employee Development and Training: Discuss examples of how companies have effectively managed employee development and training in a remote setting. Showcase initiatives such as virtual training programs, mentorship opportunities, and skill-building activities that have contributed to the professional growth of remote team members.

Employee Retention and Satisfaction: Present evidence of increased employee retention and satisfaction resulting from the adoption of embedded remote teams. Share statistics on reduced turnover rates, improved work-life balance, and surveys indicating high levels of employee contentment with the remote work arrangement.

Global Collaboration Success: Illustrate how embedded remote teams facilitate seamless collaboration across different time zones and geographical boundaries. Share stories of projects where teams from diverse locations worked cohesively, bringing together varied perspectives and skills to achieve successful outcomes.

Talent Attraction and Recruitment: Discuss how embracing remote work has enhanced companies' ability to attract top talent globally. Showcase instances where organizations have successfully recruited skilled professionals who might not have been accessible in a traditional, location-bound work model.

Adaptive Technology Integration: Explore how companies have integrated and leveraged cutting-edge technologies to enhance collaboration, communication, and project management within embedded remote teams. Highlight specific tools and platforms that have proven essential for ensuring smooth operations.

Resilience in Crisis: Examine how companies with embedded remote teams demonstrated resilience during unexpected events, such as the COVID-19 pandemic. Showcase examples where the flexibility of remote work allowed for a quick and effective response to unforeseen challenges, ensuring business continuity.

Corporate Social Responsibility (CSR): Discuss how remote work aligns with corporate social responsibility goals. Highlight instances where companies have contributed to social and community causes by, for example, supporting local initiatives, reducing commuting-related carbon footprints, and engaging in charitable activities.

Cross-Functional Collaboration:

Explore examples of how embedded remote teams have facilitated collaboration among different departments and functions within a company. Showcase instances where marketing, sales, development, and other teams seamlessly worked together, breaking down silos and fostering a more integrated organizational structure.

Customer Satisfaction and Engagement: Discuss how companies have utilized embedded remote teams to enhance customer satisfaction. Highlight instances where remote teams played a crucial role in improving customer support, implementing feedback loops, and creating personalized experiences that contribute to increased customer loyalty.

Work-Life Integration: Share stories of employees who have experienced improved work-life integration through remote work. Highlight how the flexibility of embedded remote teams allows individuals to balance professional and personal responsibilities more effectively, contributing to overall well-being.

Crisis Preparedness and Risk Mitigation: Examine how companies have used embedded remote teams as part of their crisis preparedness and risk mitigation strategies. Illustrate instances where a distributed workforce has proven beneficial in maintaining operations during unforeseen disruptions, ensuring business continuity.

Educational Initiatives: Explore how companies have implemented educational initiatives within embedded remote teams. Highlight programs that focus on up skilling and reskilling employees, promoting continuous learning, and fostering a culture of knowledge-sharing and professional development.

Tools and Technology:

Essential Remote Team Collaboration Tools: Implementing essential remote team collaboration tools is crucial for seamless communication and project coordination. These tools often include video conferencing platforms like Zoom or Microsoft Teams for virtual meetings, messaging apps such as Slack or Microsoft Teams for real-time communication, and collaborative document editing tools like Google Workspace or Microsoft 365. These tools foster efficient communication, document sharing, and collaborative workspaces essential for remote team success.

Integration of Project Management Platforms: Integrating project management platforms is vital for streamlined workflows in remote teams. Platforms like Asana, Trello, or Jira help teams organize tasks, set priorities, and monitor progress collaboratively. Integration with communication tools ensures that project discussions and task updates are easily accessible, creating a centralized hub for project-related information. This integration enhances transparency, accountability, and overall project efficiency.

Cyber security Measures for Remote Work: Implementing robust cyber security measures is imperative to safeguard sensitive data and ensure a secure remote work environment. This involves using Virtual Private Networks (VPNs) to encrypt data transmission, multifactor authentication for added login security, and endpoint protection tools to defend against malware and other cyber threats. Regular employee training on cyber security best practices, secure file-sharing protocols, and secure Wi-Fi usage contribute to a comprehensive cyber security strategy for remote teams.

Cloud-Based Storage Solutions: Utilizing cloud-based storage solutions, such as Drop box, Google Drive, or One Drive, enables remote teams to access and share files seamlessly.

These platforms provide:

- A centralized location for documents.
- Ensuring that team members can collaborate on the most up-to-date versions of files from anywhere.
- Fostering collaboration and data consistency.

Collaborative White boarding Tools: For creative collaboration and brainstorming sessions, collaborative white boarding tools like Micro or Microsoft Whiteboard can be invaluable. These tools allow team members to ideate, sketch, and share ideas in real time, replicating the experience of an in-person whiteboard session, even when team members are geographically dispersed.

Time Tracking and Productivity Tools: Implementing time tracking and productivity tools, such as Harvest or Toggle, aids in monitoring work hours, project progress, and individual productivity. These tools provide insights into time allocation, helping teams optimize their workflow and ensuring efficient use of time for remote work tasks.

Communication Protocols and Etiquette Guides: In addition to specific tools, establishing clear communication protocols and etiquette guides is essential. Define expectations for response times, preferred communication channels for different types of messages, and guidelines for virtual meetings. This ensures that remote teams can communicate effectively while respecting each other's time and preferences.

Employee Well-being Platforms: Considering the importance of well-being in a remote work environment, platforms like Headspace or Calm can be integrated to support mental health. Providing access to mindfulness and stress-relief resources contributes to a healthier and more balanced remote work experience.

Virtual Team Building Platforms: Incorporating virtual team-building platforms, like Team Bonding or Slack-based games, fosters a sense of camaraderie among remote team members. These platforms offer activities that promote teamwork, trust, and engagement, helping to build a strong team culture despite physical distances.

Employee Recognition and Rewards Systems: Implementing employee recognition and rewards systems, such as Bonuses or Kudos, is crucial for acknowledging and celebrating remote team achievements. These platforms enable team members to give each other recognition or rewards, contributing to a positive and appreciative team culture.

Automated Workflows and Zapier Integration: Utilizing automation tools and platforms like Zapier allows for the creation of seamless workflows by integrating different apps and automating repetitive tasks. This streamlines processes, reduces manual workload, and enhances overall efficiency within a remote team.

Technologies for Virtual Reality (VR) and Augmented Reality (AR): For industries where visual collaboration is key, incorporating AR and VR tools can provide immersive experiences for remote teams. Platforms like Spatial or MeetinVR enable virtual meetings in a 3D space, fostering a more interactive and engaging collaboration environment.

Learning Management Systems (LMS): Implementing Learning Management Systems, such as Module or TalentLMS, supports continuous learning and development for remote teams. These platforms facilitate the creation, delivery, and tracking of training programs, ensuring that team members can enhance their skills and knowledge remotely.

Employee Feedback and Survey Tools: Integrate tools like Survey Monkey or Culture Amp to gather regular feedback from remote team members. Conducting surveys helps gauge employee satisfaction, identify areas for improvement, and ensure that the team's needs are being addressed, fostering a culture of continuous improvement.

Language Translation Tools: For globally distributed teams, language translation tools like Google Translate or Microsoft Translator can break down language barriers, enabling effective communication and collaboration. These tools enhance inclusivity and ensure that language differences do not hinder the flow of information within the team.

Virtual Private Network (VPN) Services: Utilize reliable VPN services to secure remote team connections, especially when handling sensitive information. VPNs, like ExpressVPN or NordVPN, encrypt data transmission, providing a secure connection for remote team members working from various locations.

Digital Signature Platforms: For remote collaboration that involves document signing, implement digital signature platforms such as DocuSign or Adobe Sign. This eliminates the need for physical signatures, streamlines document workflows, and ensures the legality and security of signed agreements.

Project Analytics and Reporting Tools: Incorporate project analytics and reporting tools like Tableau or Power BI to track and analyze project performance. These tools provide valuable insights into key performance indicators, helping teams make data-driven decisions and continuously improve project outcomes.

By integrating these tools into the remote work environment, teams can enhance communication, collaboration, security, and productivity, creating a well-equipped and efficient remote workspace.

These additional tools and technologies cater to specific aspects of remote team collaboration, including team building, employee recognition, workflow automation, immersive collaboration experiences, and ongoing learning and development. Integrating this diverse set of tools contributes to a well-rounded and effective remote work environment.

The Future of Work:

As we peer into the future, the landscape of work continues to evolve. In this chapter, we'll explore emerging trends and predictions that shape the trajectory of embedded remote teams, providing insights into the next phase of the work revolution.

Hybrid Work Models: Investigate the rise of hybrid work models, blending remote and in-person collaboration. Explore how organizations strike a balance that caters to the diverse preferences and needs of their workforce.

Advancements in Virtual Reality (VR) and Augmented Reality (AR) Delve into the potential of VR and AR technologies in transforming the remote work experience. Learn how these immersive technologies can enhance collaboration and create virtual workspaces.

Focus on Employee Well-Being: Examine the growing emphasis on employee well-being in remote work scenarios. Discover wellness programs, mental health initiatives, and strategies to ensure the holistic health of remote team members.

Continuous Learning and Adaptability: Explore how the future of work demands continuous learning and adaptability. Discover how organizations foster a culture of learning, encouraging employees to up skill and stay relevant in an ever-changing landscape.

The future of work entails a shift towards embedded remote teams, leveraging trends like increased reliance on digital collaboration tools and flexible work arrangements. As technology advances, adapting to tools like AI, automation, and augmented reality becomes crucial for enhanced productivity. Finding a balance between working virtually and in-person collaboration will likely be a key challenge, requiring organizations to foster a hybrid model that optimizes both flexibility and teamwork.

Embedded remote teams are anticipated to become more prevalent, with companies emphasizing talent acquisition globally. This trend aligns with the increasing acceptance of remote work, providing access to a diverse talent pool. As technology evolves, artificial intelligence and machine learning are expected to play a larger role in automating routine tasks, enabling employees to concentrate on the more intricate and imaginative facets of their work. The future workplace is likely to witness the integration of virtual and augmented reality tools for immersive collaboration, bridging the gap between physical and remote interactions. This enhances communication and facilitates skill development and training in a virtual environment.

Balancing the advantages of remote work with the benefits of face-to-face interaction is a delicate task. Organizations may need to redefine their workplace culture and implement strategies that foster both individual autonomy and team cohesion. The future of work, therefore, revolves around embracing technological advancements while maintaining a human-centric approach to collaboration and productivity.

1) Clear Communication" in the context of leadership involves effectively conveying your vision and expectations to your team. Let's break down the components of this leadership principle:

❖ Articulating Your Vision: Clearly express the overarching goals, mission, and long-term objectives of the team or project. It aids in team members' comprehension of the goal and path, fostering a shared vision that aligns everyone toward a common goal.

- ❖ Expressing Expectations Clearly: Clearly communicate the specific duties, obligations, and performance standards for every team member when expectations are well-defined, team members clearly understand what is required, reducing ambiguity and potential misunderstandings.
- ❖ Fostering understanding: Ensure that your communication is accessible and understandable to all team members. Use language and terms that resonate with the team's diverse skill sets and backgrounds. Encourage questions and discussions to clarify any points of confusion.

- ❖ Alignment among the Team: When your vision and expectations are clearly communicated, it promotes alignment among team members. Everyone understands their contributions and how they fit into the larger picture, enhancing collaboration and synergy.

In unleashing potential, clear communication plays a vital role by providing a roadmap for team members to realize their capabilities. When expectations are transparent, individuals can better channel their efforts and talents toward achieving the team's objectives, ultimately unlocking their full potential for personal and collective success.

2) Lead by Example" is a leadership principle that underscores the importance of a leader embodying the values and work ethic they wish to see in their team. Here's a breakdown of this concept:

- ❖ Demonstrate Values: As a leader, you set the tone for the team's culture. By consistently exhibiting the values you prioritize – such as integrity, accountability, or collaboration – you establish a standard that encourages others to follow suit.

- ❖ Work Ethic: Leaders who lead by example don't just articulate expectations; they actively demonstrate a strong work ethic. It involves being diligent, committed, and dedicated to your responsibilities. When team members witness your commitment, it motivates them to invest their energy and effort into their tasks.

- ❖ Consistency: Leading by example requires consistency in your behavior. Being reliable and predictable in your actions builds trust and credibility. This consistency helps create a stable and trustworthy work environment.

❖ Inspiration: Your actions can be a source of inspiration for your team. When they see you tackling challenges with a positive attitude or going above and beyond, it encourages a similar mindset in others. Your behavior becomes a model for excellence.

❖ Alignment with Expectations: Align your conduct with the expectations you have for your team. If, for example, you emphasize punctuality, make sure you're consistently punctual yourself. This alignment reinforces the importance of the stated values and expectations.

In essence, "Lead by Example" is about being a living representation of the principles and work ethic you want your team to embrace. It's a powerful way to create a positive and high-performing work culture by inspiring your team to adopt the same standards of behavior and commitment that you exhibit.

3) Empower Your Team" is a leadership approach that involves granting team members the authority and independence to make decisions and take ownership of their work. Here's a breakdown of this leadership principle:

- Encourage autonomy: Provide team members with the freedom to act autonomously in making decisions and completing tasks. This autonomy allows individuals to leverage their skills and creativity, fostering a sense of ownership over their responsibilities.

- Decision-Making Authority: Delegate decision-making authority to capable team members. Empowering them to make choices related to their tasks or projects not only expedites the decision-making process but also promotes a proactive and engaged mindset.

- Foster Ownership: When team members feel empowered, they develop a sense of ownership and responsibility for their work. This emotional investment often leads to increased dedication and a willingness to go above and beyond to ensure success.

- Trust and confidence: Demonstrating trust in your team members' abilities builds confidence and morale. When individuals know that their leader believes in their competence, they are more likely to step up to challenges and takes initiative.

- Skill Development: Empowerment is a tool for skill development. Allowing team members to take on new responsibilities and make decisions helps them acquire new skills, broadening their professional capabilities.

- Accountability: With empowerment comes accountability. Team members understand that they are responsible for the outcomes of their decisions. This accountability promotes a sense of pride and a commitment to delivering high-quality results.

- Adaptability: Empowered teams are often more adaptable to change. When individuals are accustomed to making decisions, they become more agile and responsive to evolving circumstances.

In summary, empowering your team involves creating an environment where individuals have the freedom to act, make decisions, and take ownership of their work. It enhances individual growth and contributes to a more dynamic and high-performing team.

4) Active Listening" is a communication skill that includes paying close attention to, comprehending, and reacting to a speaker. In a leadership context, this principle emphasizes attentively engaging with your team members to build trust and enhance understanding. Here's a breakdown of this concept:

- Pay Attention: Actively listening requires giving your full attention to the person speaking. Put aside distractions, maintain eye contact, and show that you are genuinely interested in what they have to say.

- Empathy: Demonstrate empathy by trying to understand the speaker's perspective. It involves hearing their words and grasping the emotions, concerns, or enthusiasm behind their message.

- Avoid Interrupting: Resist the urge to interrupt or interject your thoughts prematurely. Allow the speaker to express themselves fully before responding. It conveys respect for their opinions and encourages open communication.

- Reflective Responses: Provide responses that reflect your understanding of what was shared. It could involve summarizing key points, asking clarifying questions, or expressing empathy. Reflective responses show that you've actively processed the information.

- Non-Verbal Cues: Make use of non-verbal clues like smiling or nodding. To signal that you are engaged in the conversation. These cues contribute to a positive and supportive communication environment.

- Seek Clarification: If something is unclear, seek clarification rather than making assumptions. It demonstrates your commitment to truly understanding the speaker's message.

- Value Feedback: Actively listening to your team's concerns, ideas, and feedback communicates that their input is valued. In turn, fosters a culture of openness and collaboration.

- Builds Trust: Active listening is a key component in building trust within a team. When team members feel heard and understood, it improves the team's relationship with the leader, creating a more supportive and cohesive work environment.

In summary, active listening goes beyond hearing words; it involves a genuine effort to understand the more profound meaning behind the communication. This practice is crucial for effective leadership, as it builds trust, enhances communication, and fosters a positive team dynamic.

5) Adaptability" in leadership refers to the ability to be open to change and to adjust strategies when necessary. It acknowledges the dynamic nature of work environments and the importance of staying flexible. Here's a breakdown of this leadership principle:

- Openness to Change: Adaptable Leaders are receptive to new ideas, evolving circumstances, and changing conditions. They understand that the business landscape is dynamic, and they are willing to embrace change rather than resist it.

- Willingness to Adjust Strategies: Adaptability involves a readiness to modify plans and strategies when the situation demands it. This flexibility allows leaders to respond effectively to unforeseen challenges or opportunities that may arise.

- Proactive Learning: Adaptable leaders are proactive learners. They seek to understand emerging trends, technologies, and industry shifts. This continuous learning mindset positions them to make informed decisions in rapidly changing environments.

- Resilience: The capacity to overcome obstacles and navigate through uncertainties is a key aspect of adaptability. Resilient leaders maintain composure during challenging times, inspiring confidence and stability within their teams.

- Effective Problem-Solving: Adaptable leaders excel at problem-solving. They can assess a situation quickly, consider alternatives, and make decisions that align with the changing circumstances. This agility is valuable in addressing unexpected challenges.

- Team Collaboration: An adaptable leader fosters a culture of flexibility within the team. It encourages team members to embrace change, contribute ideas, and collaborate on finding innovative solutions.

- Strategic Thinking: Adaptability is closely tied to strategic thinking. Leaders need to anticipate potential changes and plan accordingly. This forward-looking approach positions the team to navigate transitions more smoothly.

- Customer-Centric Approach: In industries where customer preferences or market demands evolve rapidly, an adaptable leader ensures that the team remains customer-focused. It might involve adjusting products, services, or communication strategies to meet evolving needs.

In summary, adaptability is a critical leadership trait that enables leaders to navigate uncertainty and change effectively. It involves adjusting to current circumstances and anticipating and preparing for future shifts in the business landscape.

6) Recognition and Appreciation" in leadership involves acknowledging and celebrating the achievements of team members to boost morale and motivation. Here's a breakdown of this leadership principle:

- Acknowledge Achievements: Leaders actively recognize and acknowledge the accomplishments of individuals and the team as a whole. This acknowledgment can be for reaching milestones, completing projects, or demonstrating exceptional effort.

- Timely Recognition: Providing timely recognition is crucial. Acknowledge achievements promptly to ensure that the connection between the effort exerted and the recognition given is clear. It enhances the impact of the acknowledgment.

- Personalized Recognition: Tailor your recognition efforts to individual preferences. Some team members may appreciate public acknowledgment, while others may prefer a more private form of appreciation. Knowing your team members and their preferences enhances the effectiveness of recognition.

- Celebrate Successes: Celebrate successes and milestones, whether big or small. This celebration can take various forms, such as team gatherings, shout-outs in meetings, or personalized notes of appreciation.

- Link to Values and Goals: Connect recognition to the values and goals of the team or organization. It reinforces the alignment of individual and team efforts with the overarching mission, fostering a sense of purpose.

- Motivational Impact: Recognition and appreciation serve as powerful motivators. When team members feel that their contributions are valued and acknowledged, it boosts morale, enhances job satisfaction, and encourages sustained high performance.

- Encourage a Positive Culture: A culture of recognition contributes to a positive work environment. It encourages a supportive atmosphere where team members feel appreciated and are more likely to support each other.

- Peer Recognition: Foster a culture of peer-to-peer recognition. Encourage team members to acknowledge and appreciate the efforts of their colleagues. It spreads positivity and strengthens team cohesion.

In summary, recognition and appreciation are essential components of effective leadership. Regular acknowledgment of achievements boosts morale and motivation and contributes to a positive and collaborative team culture.

7) Conflict Resolution" in leadership involves addressing conflicts promptly and diplomatically to promote a positive and collaborative work environment. Here's a breakdown of this leadership principle:

- Prompt Addressing of Conflicts: Effective conflict resolution requires dealing with issues as soon as they arise. Addressing conflicts prevents escalation and helps maintain a healthy team dynamic.

- Diplomacy and Tact: Leaders approach conflict resolution with diplomacy and Tact. It involves maintaining a calm and composed demeanor, using respectful language, and focusing on the issues at hand rather than personalizing conflicts.

- Active listening: Pay attention to the issues raised and the perspectives of all parties involved. Understanding each person's viewpoint is crucial for finding a resolution that addresses the root causes of the conflict.

- Neutral Mediation: Leaders often play the role of mediators. They should aim to remain neutral, avoiding taking sides. This neutrality builds trust among team members and ensures a fair and unbiased resolution process.

- Focus on Solutions: Encourage a solution-oriented mindset. Instead of dwelling on the problems, guide the team toward identifying constructive solutions that address the underlying issues causing the conflict.

Promote Open Communication: Establish a setting where team members may freely voice their worries. Misunderstandings are less likely to take place when there is open communication, and disagreements may be resolved before they get out of hand.

- Establish Clear Expectations: Set clear expectations for behavior and collaboration within the team. When everyone understands the expected standards, it reduces the potential for conflicts to arise.

- Follow-Up: After a resolution has been reached, follow up to ensure that the agreed-upon solutions are being implemented and that the conflict does not resurface. It demonstrates a commitment to maintaining a positive work environment.

- Provide Conflict Resolution Training: Equip team members with conflict resolution skills. Training in communication, negotiation, and conflict management can empower individuals to handle disagreements effectively.

- Promote a Positive Culture: Fostering a positive work culture where differences are respected, and conflicts are considered opportunities for growth contributes to long-term harmony within the team.

In summary, conflict resolution involves addressing conflicts proactively, employing diplomacy, and fostering a collaborative atmosphere. A leader's ability to navigate conflicts positively contributes significantly to a healthy and productive work environment.

8) Providing growth Opportunities" in leadership involves actively supporting the professional development of team members to help them grow both personally and in their careers. Here's a breakdown of this leadership principle:

- Identify Individual Goals: Understand the career aspirations and personal development goals of each team member. It involves conducting regular discussions to explore their ambitions and areas for growth.

- Tailor Development Plans: Create personalized development plans for team members based on their goals and areas of interest. These plans might include training programs, skill-building initiatives, and opportunities for hands-on experience.

- Training and Skill Enhancement: Provide access to training sessions, workshops, and resources that contribute to the acquisition of new skills or the enhancement of existing ones. It helps team members stay relevant and adaptable in their roles.

- Mentorship and Coaching: Facilitate mentorship and coaching relationships within the team. Pair less experienced team members with seasoned professionals to provide guidance, advice, and a platform for knowledge exchange.

- Promote a Culture of Continuous Learning: Encourage an ongoing learning environment. Where team members are encouraged to stay curious, explore new ideas, and seek opportunities for self-improvement. It could include supporting further education or certifications.

- Challenging Assignments: Provide challenging assignments that stretch the capabilities of team members. Assigning tasks slightly beyond their current skill level encourages growth and development.

- Feedback for Improvement: Offer constructive feedback aimed at helping team members improve. This feedback should be specific, actionable, and tied to their development goals.

- Recognition of Achievements: Acknowledge and celebrate the achievements and milestones reached by team members in their professional development. Recognition reinforces the value of their efforts and motivates further growth.

- Promotion Opportunities: Actively consider team members for promotion opportunities when they demonstrate readiness for increased responsibilities. It signals that growth and advancement are recognized and rewarded within the organization.

- Provide Resources: Ensure that team members have access to the necessary resources, both financial and informational, to pursue their professional development goals.

In summary, providing growth opportunities involves a proactive approach to nurturing the professional development of team members. By investing in their growth, leaders contribute to the overall success of the team while fostering a culture of continuous learning and improvement.

9) Decision-making skills" in leadership involve the ability to make well-informed and timely decisions, considering relevant input, especially from the team. Here's a breakdown of this leadership principle:

- Well-Informed Decisions: Leaders should gather and analyze relevant information before making decisions. It involves seeking data, insights, and perspectives to ensure a comprehensive understanding of the situation at hand.

- Consider Team Input: Effective leaders recognize the value of diverse perspectives. They involve their team in the decision-making process, especially when the decision impacts the team directly. This inclusion can lead to more well-rounded decisions and fosters a collaborative environment.

10) **Timely Decision-Making:** While it's important to gather sufficient information, leaders must also make decisions in a timely manner. Delayed decision-making can hinder progress and create uncertainty. Striking the right balance between thoroughness and timeliness is crucial.

- Risk Assessment: Decision-making involves assessing potential risks and benefits. Leaders should be adept at weighing the potential outcomes of different choices, considering both short-term and long-term implications.

- Adaptability: Effective decision-makers are adaptable. They can adjust their strategies and choices in response to changing circumstances. This flexibility is vital in dynamic and unpredictable environments.

- Clear Communication: After deciding, leaders should communicate it clearly to the team. Transparency helps team members understand the rationale behind decisions, promoting a sense of clarity and alignment.

11) **Accountability:** Leaders take accountability for their decisions. Whether the outcome is positive or negative, taking responsibility fosters trust and demonstrates leadership integrity.

- Decisiveness: Being decisive is a key aspect of decision-making skills. It involves the ability to make tough choices even in ambiguous or high-pressure situations.

Decisiveness is often associated with confidence and leadership authority.

- Learning from decisions: Effective leaders see decisions, whether successful or not, as learning opportunities. They assess outcomes, identify lessons, and use this knowledge to inform future decision-making processes.

- Strategic Decision-Making: Leaders align decisions with the broader strategic goals of the organization. It ensures that individual choices contribute to the overall success and direction of the team or company.

In summary, decision-making skills involve a combination of analytical thinking, collaboration, and a strategic approach. Leaders who excel in this area can navigate complex situations, inspire confidence, and drive their teams toward success.

12) The capacity to appreciate people on a profound level" in initiative alludes to the capacity to comprehend and oversee both your feelings and the feelings of your colleagues, fully intent on encouraging an amicable work environment. Here is a breakdown of this initiative rule:

- Self-Awareness: Pioneers with the ability to understand people on a profound level are receptive to their feelings. They perceive how they feel and comprehend the effect of these feelings on their way of behaving and direction.

- Self-Regulation: This includes the capacity to actually oversee and get a handle on one's feelings. Pioneers with a high ability to understand anyone on a deeper level can stay created and pursue sane choices, even in testing or high-pressure circumstances.

- Empathy: Pioneers who can appreciate individuals on a profound level can comprehend and discuss the thoughts of others. It includes being sensitive to the feelings of colleagues, showing sympathy, and taking into account their points of view in navigation.

- Effective Communication: The capacity to appreciate individuals on a profound level improves relational abilities. Pioneers can communicate their feelings plainly and grasp the close-to-home signals of others, prompting more viable and sympathetic correspondence.

- Motivation: Pioneers with the ability to understand people at their core are, much of the time, self-propelled and can motivate others. They have a reasonable feeling of direction and can convey excitement, which adds to a good and roused group climate.

- Social Skills: Solid interactive abilities are a part of the capacity to understand individuals at their core. It includes exploring social circumstances successfully, building positive connections, and encouraging a cooperative and strong group culture.

- Conflict Resolution: Pioneers with the ability to understand people on a profound level succeed in settling clashes strategically. They comprehend the feelings engaged with clashes, stay fair-minded, and guide the group toward the goal in a productive way.

- Adaptability: Sincerely, smart pioneers are versatile despite change. They can explore vulnerabilities and assist their colleagues with adapting to change by understanding and tending to their feelings.

- Cultural Sensitivity: The ability to understand people at their core stretches out to perceiving and regarding social contrasts. Pioneers with this range of abilities value the different close-to-home articulations and correspondence styles inside a multicultural group.

- Building Trust: The ability to appreciate people on a deeper level adds to the structure of trust. At the point when colleagues feel comprehended and esteemed, trust is reinforced, making an establishment for an amicable and cooperative working environment.

In rundown, the capacity to understand people on a deeper level is an essential initiative expertise that adds to making a positive and amicable work environment. Pioneers who get it and deal with feelings really can explore complex relational elements, rouse their groups, and encourage a sound workplace.

13) Continuous Learning" in leadership involves fostering a culture that encourages ongoing learning and improvement, both for the leader and the team. Here's a breakdown of this leadership principle:

- Personal Development: Leaders who value continuous learning prioritize their professional development. It involves seeking new knowledge, staying updated on industry trends, and refining leadership skills through self-directed learning, courses, or workshops.

- Modeling Behavior: Leaders set the tone for the team. By actively engaging in continuous learning, leaders model the importance of staying curious and adaptable. This behavior can inspire team members to embrace a similar mindset.

- Providing Learning Opportunities: Actively support and provide opportunities for the professional development of team members. It could include access to training programs, workshops, conferences, or mentorship initiatives.

- Skill Enhancement: Encourage the acquisition and enhancement of skills relevant to individual roles within the team. Leaders should identify skill gaps and work collaboratively with team members to address them through targeted learning opportunities.

- Knowledge Sharing: Facilitate a culture of knowledge sharing within the team. Encourage team members to share insights, best practices, and lessons learned. This collaborative approach contributes to collective learning and growth.

- Feedback for Improvement: Provide constructive feedback aimed at promoting continuous improvement. This feedback should be specific, actionable, and tied to both individual and team goals.

- Adapting to Change: Continuous learning fosters adaptability. Team members who are committed to learning are better capable of successfully adjusting to changes in the work environment, whether they be technological advancements or shifts in industry practices.

- Innovation: A culture of continuous learning supports innovation. Team members who are encouraged to explore new ideas and approaches contribute to a dynamic and innovative work environment.

- Performance Metrics: Establish performance metrics that reflect a commitment to continuous learning. Recognize and reward team members who actively engage in professional development and contribute to the learning culture.

- Reflection and Growth Mindset: Encourage a mindset of reflection and continuous improvement. Leaders and team members alike should view challenges as opportunities to learn and grow, promoting resilience and adaptability.

In summary, continuous learning is a dynamic and integral aspect of effective leadership. Leaders who prioritize learning contribute to a workplace culture that values growth, innovation, and the ongoing development of both individual team members and the team as a whole.

14) Time Management" in leadership involves the effective prioritization of tasks and assisting the team in managing their time efficiently to maximize overall productivity. Here's a breakdown of this leadership principle:

- Task Prioritization: Leaders need to identify and prioritize tasks based on their urgency and importance. It involves distinguishing between tasks that require immediate attention and those that contribute to long-term goals.

- Setting Clear Goals: Clearly defined goals provide a framework for task prioritization. Leaders should work with the team to establish specific, measurable, and achievable goals, helping everyone understand the overall objectives.

- Effective Delegation: Delegating tasks according to team members' strengths and capabilities is a crucial aspect of time management. Leaders should empower team members to take ownership of specific responsibilities.

- Time Blocking: Encourage the use of time-blocking techniques, where specific blocks of time are allocated to focus on particular tasks or projects. It helps minimize distractions and enhances concentration.

- Utilizing technology: Leaders can introduce or recommend tools and technologies that aid in time management, such as project management software, communication platforms, and scheduling applications.

- Regular Check-Ins: Schedule regular check-ins to assess progress on tasks and projects. It allows leaders to provide guidance, identify potential roadblocks, and make adjustments to prioritize if needed.

- Setting Realistic Deadlines: Establish realistic deadlines for tasks, considering the complexity of the work and the resources available. Unrealistic timelines can lead to stress and decreased overall productivity.

- Encouraging Breaks: recognize the importance of breaks for maintaining focus and productivity. Encourage short breaks to recharge and avoid burnout, as sustained periods of intense work can be counterproductive.

- Time Management Training: Provide training or resources on effective time management techniques for the team. It can include workshops, seminars, or access to relevant literature on optimizing work processes.

- Flexibility and Adaptability: Recognize that unexpected challenges and changes may occur. Leaders should guide the team in remaining flexible and adaptable to ensure effective time management in dynamic environments.

In summary, effective time management in leadership involves a combination of strategic planning, effective delegation, technology utilization, and a commitment to ongoing improvement. By optimizing time usage, leaders contribute to a more productive and efficient work environment for the entire team.

15) Promote Collaboration" in leadership involves creating an environment that encourages team members to share ideas, work together on projects, and leverage each other's strengths. Here's a breakdown of this leadership principle:

Encourage open communication to foster an atmosphere where team members are at ease with open communication. Expressing their ideas, opinions, and concerns. This open dialogue fosters a foundation for collaboration.

- **Encouraging idea Sharing:** Actively encourage team members to share their ideas and insights. It can be done through regular team meetings, brainstorming sessions, or dedicated platforms for idea exchange.

- **Team Building Activities:** Organize team-building activities that promote interaction and strengthen relationships among team members. It could include workshops, off-site events, or collaborative projects.

- **Recognizing Diverse Strengths:** Acknowledge and appreciate the diverse abilities and strengths that every team member contributes. Understanding and leveraging these strengths contributes to a more effective and well-rounded team.

- **Cross-Functional Collaboration:** Encourage collaboration across different departments or functional areas. This cross-functional collaboration can lead to innovative solutions and a more comprehensive approach to projects.

- **Providing Collaborative Tools**: Equip the team with the necessary tools and technologies to facilitate collaboration. It could include project management software, communication platforms, and file-sharing systems.

- **Facilitating Team Workshops:** Conduct workshops or training sessions focused on enhancing collaboration skills. It could involve team-building exercises, communication training, or workshops on effective collaboration techniques.

- **Setting Clear Goals:** Clearly define team goals and objectives. When everyone understands the collective mission, it fosters cooperation and a feeling of purpose among participants toward common objectives.

- **Recognition of Collaborative Efforts:** Recognize and celebrate instances of successful collaboration. This acknowledgment reinforces the value of teamwork and encourages continued collaboration among team members.

- **Lead by Example:** Demonstrate a collaborative mindset through your actions. Leaders who actively participate in collaborative efforts set a precedent for the team, reinforcing the importance of working together.

In summary, promoting collaboration involves creating a supportive environment where team members feel empowered to collaborate, share ideas, and contribute to collective success. Leaders play a vital part in encouraging this cooperative culture by setting expectations, providing resources, and leading by example.

16) Encourage Risk-Taking" in leadership involves fostering a culture where calculated risks are welcomed, enabling team members to step outside their comfort zones and innovate. Here's a breakdown of this leadership principle:

- Define a Safe Environment: Clarify that the team operates in a safe and supportive environment where taking

calculated risks is encouraged. Team members should feel
secure in expressing new ideas and exploring innovative
approaches.

- Clarify the Difference between Calculated and Reckless
  Risks: emphasize the importance of calculated risks – those
  based on thorough analysis and understanding of potential
  outcomes. Distinguish between thoughtful, strategic risk-
  taking and impulsive or reckless behavior.

- Learning from Failure: Instill a mindset that sees failure as
  a chance for growth and development rather than a negative
  outcome. Encourage team members to analyze failures,
  extract lessons, and apply these insights to future
  endeavors.

- Provide Resources and Support: offer the necessary
  resources and support for team members to explore new
  ideas. It might include training, mentorship, or access to
  tools and technologies that facilitate innovation.

- Celebrate Innovation: Recognize and celebrate instances of
  successful risk-taking and innovation. This
  acknowledgment reinforces the value of creativity and

encourages a culture where individuals are willing to push boundaries.

- Promote Entrepreneurship: Encourage entrepreneurial activities within the team – initiatives that operate like entrepreneurial ventures within the confines of the organization. It allows team members to explore and develop new ideas with a degree of autonomy.

- Establish a Feedback Loop: Create a feedback mechanism that allows team members to share insights, challenges, and outcomes of their risk-taking endeavors. This feedback loop promotes continuous improvement and informs future decision-making.

- Set an Example: Leaders should lead by example, demonstrating a willingness to take calculated risks themselves. When team members see their leaders embracing innovation, they are more likely to follow suit.

- Balance and Alignment: Help team members strike a balance between risk and alignment with organizational goals. Ensure that innovative efforts align with the broader mission and vision while encouraging creative thinking.

- Promote an environment where team members are always improving constantly looking for better methods to accomplish objectives. This mindset supports ongoing innovation and the exploration of new possibilities.

In summary, encouraging risk-taking involves creating an environment that values innovation, learning from experimentation, and strategically pushing boundaries. Leaders play a pivotal role in shaping this culture by providing support, celebrating successes, and fostering a mindset that views calculated risks as essential for growth and progress.

17) Inspire a Growth Mindset" in leadership involves cultivating a culture within the team that emphasizes the conviction that aptitudes may be enhanced by commitment and diligence. Here's a breakdown of this leadership principle:

- The conviction that aptitudes may be enhanced by commitment and diligence. It involves encouraging curiosity, providing opportunities for skill development, and promoting a positive attitude toward challenges.

- Model a Growth Mindset: Leaders should exemplify a growth mindset by embracing challenges, persisting through setbacks, and actively seeking opportunities for learning and development. Modeling this mindset sets a powerful example for the team.

- Encourage Effort and Persistence: emphasize the importance of effort and persistence over innate talent. Encourage team members to see challenges as opportunities for growth rather than as indicators of limitations.

- Acknowledge and Celebrate progress: Recognize and celebrate individual and team progress. Acknowledging incremental improvements reinforces the idea that growth is a continuous process and should be appreciated at every stage.

- Provide Constructive Feedback: Offer feedback that is constructive and focused on areas for improvement. Frame feedback in a way that encourages team members to see it as valuable input for growth rather than criticism.

- Promote Skill Development: Encourage team members to actively seek opportunities for skill development. It might involve training programs, workshops, or mentorship initiatives aimed at expanding their professional capabilities.

- Normalize Setbacks as Learning Opportunities: Reinforce the idea that setbacks are a natural part of the learning process. Help the team view failures as opportunities to learn, adapt, and ultimately grow stronger.

- Create a Culture of Collaboration: A growth mindset is often fostered in collaborative environments. Encourage teamwork, knowledge-sharing, and mentorship to facilitate a culture where team members support each other's development.

- Set Stretch Goals: Encourage the team to set stretch goals that challenge their current abilities. These goals should be ambitious yet achievable with effort and dedication, promoting a mindset of continuous improvement.

- Provide Learning Resources: Equip the team with resources that support ongoing learning. It could include access to educational materials, workshops, or platforms that facilitate skill-building and professional development.

In summary, inspiring a growth mindset involves creating a culture that values learning, effort, and resilience. Leaders play a pivotal role in shaping this mindset by modeling the desired behavior, providing support, and reinforcing the belief that individuals and teams can continually develop and improve.

Ensuring Employee Well-Being:

In this chapter, we'll delve into the critical aspect of prioritizing the well-being of embedded remote team members. As the professional landscape shifts, organizations must proactively address the challenges that remote work can pose to mental and physical health.

Wellness Programs

Wellness programs are organized initiatives within workplaces designed to promote and support the overall health and well-being of employees. These programs typically encompass a variety of strategies intended to enhance one's emotional, mental, and physical well-being. Here are some common elements:

1. **Physical Health:** Providing resources and activities that encourage physical activity, such as gym memberships, fitness challenges, or on-site exercise classes. This may also include initiatives to promote healthy eating habits and weight management.

2. **Mental Health:** Offering support services such as counseling, stress management training, mindfulness sessions, or workshops aimed at reducing stress and enhancing mental well-being.

3. **Health Screenings:** Arranging periodic health check-ups or screenings to detect health issues early and promote preventive healthcare.

4. **Education and Awareness:** Organizing workshops, seminars, or providing resources on various health topics like nutrition, exercise, mental health, and overall well-being.

5. **Smoking Cessation Programs:** Supporting employees who want to quit smoking by offering resources, counseling, or cessation programs.

6. **Financial Wellness:** Including information, workshops, or support services aimed at helping employees manage their

financial well-being, including budgeting, investment, and retirement planning.

7. **Work-Life Balance:** Promoting programs or policies that support a healthy balance between work and personal life, such as flexible work hours or remote work options.

8. Offering incentives and rewards: Providing prizes or incentives for participating in wellness activities or achieving health-related goals.

Wellness programs aim to create a supportive environment that values and prioritizes the health of employees. By addressing various aspects of well-being, these programs contribute to increased employee morale, improved health outcomes, and a more positive and productive work environment.

Mental Health Support for Remote Workers

Mental health support for remote workers is crucial, considering the unique challenges associated with remote work. Here are strategies and resources to address mental health concerns:

- Virtual Counseling Services: Offer remote access to counseling services through video calls or teletherapy to provide confidential and professional mental health support

- Employee Assistance Programs (EAPs): Provide resources like EAPs, offering confidential counseling, financial advice, and legal support to help employees navigate personal challenges.

- Stress Management Workshops: Conduct virtual workshops on stress management techniques, including mindfulness, meditation, and relaxation exercises.

- Flexible Work Hours: Allow flexibility in work hours to accommodate various personal schedules and promote a better work-life balance, reducing stress.

- Regular Check-ins: Schedule regular one-on-one check-ins between managers and team members to discuss work challenges, address concerns, and provide emotional support.

- Virtual Mental Health Resources: Share resources such as articles, videos, and webinars on mental health topics to raise awareness and provide education.

- Encourage Breaks: Remind employees to take regular to prevent burnout, take pauses and get away from their desks and maintain mental well-being.

- Social Connection Initiatives: Facilitate virtual social activities, team-building exercises, or informal online gatherings to foster a sense of community and combat feelings of isolation.

- Clear Communication: Ensure transparent and empathetic communication, keeping employees informed about changes and expectations and providing reassurance during uncertain times.

- Promote Boundaries: Encourage setting clear boundaries between work and personal life to prevent remote workers from feeling constantly "on."

By addressing the mental health needs of remote workers, organizations can create a supportive work environment that contributes to overall well-being and job satisfaction.

- ***Promoting Work-Life Integration***

Promoting work-life integration emphasizes creating a harmonious balance between professional responsibilities and personal well-being. Key points include:

- Holistic Well-Being: Recognize that employees have lives outside of work and aim to support their overall well-being, acknowledging the interconnectedness of work and personal life.

- Flexible Working Arrangements: Offer flexibility in working hours or remote work options, allowing employees to better integrate work with family, personal interests, and other aspects of their lives

- Clear Expectations: Set clear expectations regarding working hours, deadlines, and communication norms to help employees manage their time effectively.

- Respecting Downtime: Encourage a culture that respects downtime, avoiding after-hours emails or messages to allow employees to unwind and recharge.

- Supporting Parental Responsibilities: Acknowledge and support employees with parental responsibilities by offering parental leave, flexible schedules, or childcare assistance.

- Well-Defined Breaks: Encourage employees to take regular breaks during the workday, promoting mental refreshment and preventing burnout.

- Maintain open lines of communication: Create a welcoming atmosphere for staff members to communicate their needs regarding work-life integration, encouraging open dialogue.

- Technology Boundaries: Establish guidelines on the use of technology after working hours to prevent constant connectivity and help employees detach from work when required.

- Employee Recognition: Acknowledge and appreciate employees for their efforts and achievements, promoting a positive work environment that enhances job satisfaction.

By promoting work-life integration, organizations contribute to a healthier and more sustainable work culture, ultimately benefiting both employees and the overall success of the business.

Flexibility in Scheduling

Flexibility in scheduling acknowledges the importance of empowering employees to manage their time effectively while accommodating personal commitments. Key considerations include:

- Autonomy and Empowerment: Providing flexibility in work schedules empowers employees to take control of their time, fostering a sense of autonomy and responsibility.

- Balancing Personal and Professional Commitments: Flexible schedules allow employees to better balance personal obligations, such as childcare, appointments, or other non work responsibilities, without compromising work performance.

- Increased Job Satisfaction: Flexibility is often associated with higher job satisfaction, as it acknowledges the diverse needs and preferences of employees, contributing to a positive work environment.

- Improved Work-Life Balance: Flexible schedules support a healthier work-life balance, reducing stress and preventing burnout by allowing employees to adapt their work hours to suit their lifestyle.

- Attracting and Retaining Talent: Organizations that prioritize flexibility are more likely to attract and retain top talent, as it demonstrates a commitment to employee well-being and work-life integration.

- Customization of Work Hours: Allowing employees to customize their work hours based on their peak productivity times can lead to better performance and job satisfaction.

- Remote Work Opportunities: Enabling remote work options provides an additional layer of flexibility, allowing employees to work from different locations that suit their needs.

- Clear Communication: Establish clear guidelines and communication channels to ensure that flexibility does not compromise teamwork or project timelines.

- Performance-Based Evaluation: Shift the focus from traditional "time spent at the desk" to evaluating employee performance based on outcomes and contributions.

By embracing flexibility in scheduling, organizations create a work culture that values individual needs, leading to increased employee satisfaction, productivity, and retention.

- ***Encouraging Social Connections***

Encouraging social connections in the workplace involves fostering a setting where workers may forge relationships and form social bonds with their colleagues. Here's how it typically operates:

1. **Team Building Activities:** Organizing team-building exercises, workshops, or social events that allow employees to engage with one another in a more relaxed setting. These activities can range from group outings to casual team lunches or games.

2. **Open Workspaces:** Designing workspaces that encourage interaction and collaboration. This might involve open office layouts, communal areas, or shared spaces where employees can connect and converse more easily.

3. Staff Resource Groups: Promoting the establishment of staff resources or interest groups within the company. These groups can focus on shared interests, hobbies, or diverse cultural backgrounds, fostering a sense of community.

4. **Mentorship Programs:** Establishing mentorship initiatives where experienced employees can connect with and support newer or less experienced colleagues, creating opportunities for social connections and learning.

5. **Social Events:** Hosting regular social events or gatherings, such as holiday parties, team dinners, or celebrations for

milestones or achievements, allowing employees to connect in a more informal setting.

6. **Cross-Departmental Collaboration:** Encouraging collaboration between different departments or teams on projects or initiatives. This allows employees to interact with colleagues they might not typically work with, fostering new connections.

7. **Supportive Culture:** Creating a culture that values social connections, where employees feel comfortable engaging with one another, sharing ideas, and forming friendships within the workplace.

Encouraging social connections in the workplace can lead to improved teamwork, increased job satisfaction, and a more positive work environment. It also contributes to higher morale, better communication, and a stronger sense of belonging among employees.

- ***Providing Resources for Remote Ergonomics***

Providing resources for remote ergonomics involves offering guidance, tools, and support to ensure that employees working have a comfortable and ergonomically sound workspace. Here's how it works:

1. **Guidelines and Recommendations:** Distributing information and guidelines on how to set up an ergonomic

workstation at home. This could include proper desk and chair height, monitor positioning, and the importance of good posture.

2. **Equipment Provision:** Offering or subsidizing ergonomic furniture and accessories, such as adjustable chairs, standing desks, ergonomic keyboards, and mo

3. Use pads, to support a healthier work environment at home.

4. **Training and Education:** Conducting workshops or training sessions on remote ergonomics, teaching employees how to adjust their home workspace for optimal comfort and health.

5. **Online Resources:** Providing access to online resources, videos, or articles that offer tips and guidance on setting up a home office ergonomically.

6. **Consultation Services:** Offering remote consultations or assessments by ergonomics specialists to help employees customize their workspace based on individual needs.

7. **Regular Check-ins:** Periodic follow-ups to ensure employees are comfortable with their setup and addressing any concerns or issues they might be facing with their remote workspace.

Ensuring proper ergonomic setups for remote work helps reduce the risk of work-related musculoskeletal disorders, enhances employee well-being, and contributes to better productivity and job satisfaction. It's about creating an environment where employees working from home can maintain their health and comfort as they work.

Open Communication

Open communication refers to a workplace a setting in which staff members feel free to voice their opinions and concerns. It involves creating a culture where individuals can voice their opinions, share feedback, and engage in transparent conversations. Here's how it typically operates:

1. **Accessibility to Information:** Open communication ensures that relevant information is accessible to employees. This could include company updates, policies, and changes within the organization, enabling everyone to be informed.

2. **Encouraging Dialogue:** Employees are encouraged to express their thoughts, pose inquiries, and provide criticism without worrying about retaliation. This includes both upward communication to management and lateral communication among colleagues.

3. **Active Listening:** It involves not only speaking openly but also actively listening to others. This fosters a culture where everyone feels heard and respected.

4. **Constructive Feedback:** Encourages giving and receiving constructive criticism. It's about providing feedback in a way that helps individuals improve without discouraging their initiative or enthusiasm.

5. **Transparency:** Open communication emphasizes honesty and transparency in interactions, particularly when discussing issues that impact the team or organization.

6. **Conflict Resolution:** Encourages open dialogue to address conflicts and issues that may arise in the workplace, ensuring that concerns are dealt with openly and professionally.

7. **Inclusivity and Diversity:** Open communication celebrates and respects different perspectives, encouraging a diverse range of voices and experiences to be heard and valued.

8. **Clear Channels:** It involves establishing clear channels for communication, ensuring that information flows effectively, and that there are platforms for open discussions, such as meetings, feedback sessions, or suggestion boxes.

By fostering open communication, organizations can benefit from improved problem-solving, innovation, trust, and a more positive work culture. It fosters a culture in which workers feel empowered and appreciated leading to higher engagement and productivity.

- **Team Building:**

Team building involves a series of activities or strategies designed to foster cohesion, collaboration, and trust among members of a group, with the aim of improving their collective performance. Here's how it typically works:

1. **Building Relationships:** Activities are structured to help team members get to know each other better, both professionally and personally. This might involve icebreakers, team lunches, or social events.

2. **Improving Communication:** Team-building exercises often focus on enhancing communication among team members. This could involve problem-solving tasks, group projects, or role-playing scenarios that encourage effective interaction.

3. **Developing Trust:** Activities are designed to build trust among team members. Trust is crucial for teamwork, so exercises that require cooperation and reliance on one another are common.

4. **Identifying Strengths and Weaknesses:** Team-building activities can highlight individual strengths and weaknesses, helping team members understand how they can complement each other's skills and work more effectively as a group.

5. **Enhancing Collaboration:** Encouraging teamwork and collaboration is a fundamental aspect of team building. This can involve tasks that require joint decision-making, problem-solving, or strategizing.

6. **Creating a Supportive Environment:** Team building fosters a culture of support where team members feel comfortable asking for help, sharing ideas, and contributing to collective goals.

7. **Improving Morale and Motivation:** Engaging in team-building activities often leads to increased morale, motivation, and a sense of belonging, contributing to a positive work culture.

8. **Encouraging Creativity and Innovation:** Some team-building exercises are designed to stimulate creativity and innovative thinking, helping teams approach challenges with fresh perspectives.

Effective team building is an ongoing process that requires a variety of activities tailored to the needs and dynamics of the team.

When done well, it can significantly improve team performance, productivity, and overall job satisfaction.

Wellness Programs:

Wellness programs involve implementing initiatives to support and improve the overall well-being of employees. Key components include:

- Fitness Challenges: Organize challenges that encourage physical activity, such as step challenges, virtual races, or workout competitions. It promotes a more active lifestyle among employees.

- Nutritional Workshops: Conduct workshops or seminars on nutrition, healthy eating habits, and the importance of a balanced diet. Provide practical tips for making nutritious food choices.

- Mindfulness Sessions: Offer mindfulness and stress reduction sessions, including guided meditation, deep-breathing exercises, or yoga. These activities help employees manage stress and enhance mental well-being.

- Health Screenings: Provide opportunities for health screenings to monitor key indicators like blood pressure, cholesterol levels, or body mass index. It can raise awareness of individual health and risk factors.

- Employee Assistance Programs (EAPs): Implement EAPs that offer confidential counseling and support services for employees facing personal or professional challenges.

- Well-being Challenges: Create challenges that focus on overall well-being, incorporating aspects of physical, mental, and emotional health. Examples include sleep improvement challenges or stress reduction programs.

- Financial Wellness Workshops: Address the financial well-being of employees by organizing workshops on budgeting, financial planning, and investment strategies.

- Community Engagement: Encourage employees to participate in community service or volunteer programs, fostering a sense of purpose and community.

- Customized Wellness Plans: Provide personalized wellness plans based on individual needs and preferences, acknowledging that well-being are unique to each employee.

Implementing comprehensive wellness programs contributes to a positive workplace culture, promotes a healthier lifestyle, and can lead to increased employee satisfaction and productivity.

- Remote work considerations involve providing essential support and resources for employees working outside the traditional office setting. Key aspects include:

- Technical Support: Ensure that remote employees have the necessary tools, software, and technical support to carry out their tasks efficiently.

- Home Office Setup: Offer guidance on setting up a comfortable and ergonomically sound home office, including recommendations for furniture, lighting, and equipment.

- Communication Platforms: Implement reliable communication platforms for virtual meetings, collaboration, and efficient information exchange among remote team members.

- Training and Development: Provide resources for ongoing training and professional development, ensuring that remote employees have access to learning opportunities that contribute to their career growth.

- Flexible Schedules: recognize the importance of flexibility in work hours to accommodate various time zones, personal preferences, and individual productivity peaks.

- Mental Health Support: Offer resources such as counseling services, stress management programs, and mental health initiatives to address the potential challenges associated with remote work.

- Clear Expectations: Set clear expectations regarding work responsibilities, deadlines, and communication norms to help remote employees navigate their roles effectively.

- Security Measures: Implement robust cybersecurity measures to protect sensitive information and ensure the secure exchange of data in a remote work environment.

- Collaborative Tools: Provide access to collaborative tools and platforms that facilitate seamless teamwork and project management, enhancing productivity for remote teams.

- Regular Check-ins: Schedule regular virtual check-ins between managers and team members to discuss work progress, address concerns, and maintain a sense of connection.

Addressing these considerations ensures that employees have the necessary resources and support to thrive in their roles, contributing to overall job satisfaction and success in a virtual work environment.

Inclusive Policies:

Establish policies that promote diversity, equity, and inclusion, ensuring all employees feel valued and respected. Comprehensive strategies are hierarchical rules intended to advance variety, value, and consideration (DEI) inside the working environment. Key parts include:

Diversity: Empower a different labor force by effectively looking for and embracing people from different foundations, including various identities, sexual orientations, ages, capacities, and points of view.

- Equity: Guarantee decency and equivalent open doors for all representatives, recognizing and tending to foundational hindrances that might obstruct the expert development of specific gatherings.

- Inclusion: Cultivate a culture where each representative feels included, esteemed, and regarded, independent of their experience. It includes establishing a climate where people can contribute their novel points of view, unafraid of segregation.

- Anti-Segregation Policies: Lay out clear arrangements that expressly preclude separation considering race, orientation, sexual direction, religion, or some other safeguarded trademark.

- Training and Education: Preparing projects to bring issues to light about oblivious inclinations, advance social ability, and improve comprehension of DEI issues.

- Accessible Offices and Technology: Guarantee that working environment offices and innovation are available to all representatives, incorporating those with handicaps, to establish a comprehensive climate.

- Flexible Work Policies: Execute adaptable work arrangements that oblige different requirements, like remote work choices or adaptable timetables, recognizing the changed conditions of representatives.

- Diverse Authority Representation: Energize variety in positions of authority to mirror the structure of the more extensive labor force, giving good examples and separating boundaries.

- Feedback Mechanisms: Lay out systems for representatives to give input on the inclusivity of the work environment, considering ceaseless improvement and responsiveness to representative worries.

- Support for Representative Asset Groups: Energize and uphold the development of worker asset bunches that emphasize unambiguous parts of variety, giving a stage for shared encounters and support.

Comprehensive strategies add to a positive working environment culture as well as improve inventiveness, development, and, in general, hierarchical accomplishment by utilizing the qualities of a different and comprehensive labor force.

Ergonomics

This Includes planning and organizing the work area to fit the requirements of the specialist, stressing solace, effectiveness, and well-being. Key parts of ergonomic standards to upgrade work areas include:

- Work area Design: Organize work areas, seats, and gear in a way that advances a characteristic and agreeable body act. It diminishes the gamble of outer muscle issues like back torment or dull strain wounds.

- Seat and Work Area Setup: Pick movable seats and work areas that permit representatives to keep up with legitimate stances. Guarantee that the work area level, seat level, and screen position support an impartial body arrangement.

- PC Screen Placement: Position screens at eye level and at a safe distance to lessen eye strain and forestall neck and shoulder distress. Utilize a flexible screen stand if necessary.

- Console and Mouse Placement: Keep the console and mouse at a level that permits the lower arms to be lined up with the floor. These limit the burden on the wrists and lessen the gamble of conditions like carpal passage disorder.

- Lighting: Give satisfactory and customizable lighting to diminish eye strain. Keep away from glare on screens and guarantee that the lighting is even across the work area.

- Incessant Breaks: Urge representatives to enjoy short reprieves and stretch consistently to forestall firmness and keep up with dissemination.

- Legitimate Seat Support: Select seats with legitimate lumbar help to keep up with the normal bend of the spine. Customizable seats with armrests generally add to the comfort.

- Link Management: Keep links coordinated and far removed to forestall stumbling risks and keep a messiness-free work area.

- Ergonomic Accessories: Give ergonomic embellishments like ergonomic consoles, mice, and hassocks to help create a more agreeable and effective workplace.

- Preparing and Education: Teach representatives about the significance of ergonomics and give preparation on the most proficient method to set up their workstations accurately to limit the gamble of actual distress and wounds.

By integrating ergonomic standards into the plan and arrangement of work areas, associations can add to the general prosperity of representatives and diminish the probability of business-related wounds and inconvenience.

Financial Well-Being:

Offer financial wellness programs or resources to assist employees in managing their finances effectively. Monetary prosperity drives include giving projects and assets to assist representatives with dealing with their funds, actually. Key parts include:

- Financial Schooling Workshops: Lead studios or classes on planning, saving, effective money management, and the obligation of the executives to improve representatives' monetary proficiency.

- Retirement Arranging Assistance: Offer data and assets to assist representatives with making arrangements for their retirement remembering the direction for business-supported retirement plans and individual retirement accounts (IRAs).

- Financial Counseling: Give admittance to monetary guiding administrations where representatives can look for customized exhortation on overseeing obligation, making a spending plan, or tending to explicit monetary difficulties.

- Employee Help Projects (EAPs): Coordinate monetary prosperity into more extensive EAPs, offering comprehensive help that incorporates monetary guidance alongside psychological well-being and other help.

- Student Advance Assistance: Execute programs that help workers in overseeing understudy loan obligations, for example, giving data on reimbursement choices or offering boss commitments.

- Savings and Speculation Programs: Urge workers to save and contribute through business-supported programs, such as matching commitments to retirement records or stock buy plans.

- Emergency Asset Support: Advance the significance of building and keeping up with crisis assets to assist workers with exploring unforeseen monetary difficulties.

- Debt Reimbursement Strategies: Offer direction on procedures for overseeing and paying off past commitments, including Visa obligations, advances, and other monetary commitments.

- Financial Wellbeing Platforms: Give admittance to online stages or applications that offer monetary apparatuses, assets, and instructive substance to help representatives settle on informed monetary choices.

- Flexible Remuneration Packages: Investigate choices for adaptable pay bundles that permit representatives to modify benefits in light of their monetary necessities.

By tending to monetary prosperity, associations add to the general well-being and solidness of their representatives, encouraging a more connected and centered labor force. Monetarily secure representatives are better prepared to oversee pressure and spotlight their expert obligations

Feedback and Improvement:

Feedback and improvement strategies in the workplace involve creating a system where constructive input is given and received to enhance performance, productivity, and overall professional development. Here's how these strategies typically work:

1. **Regular Feedback:** Establishing a culture of regular feedback, both formal (such as performance appraisals) and informal (like ongoing conversations), is vital. It provides employees with a consistent understanding of their progress and areas for improvement.

2. **Constructive Criticism:** Feedback should be constructive, highlighting both strengths and areas for development. It should focus on behaviors and actions rather than personal characteristics.

3. **Goal Setting:** Align feedback with individual or team goals. By setting clear objectives, feedback becomes more purposeful and helps direct efforts toward specific improvements.

4. **Two-Way Communication:** Encourage open dialogue. Workers should be at ease giving supervisors and fellow staff members feedback. This encourages creativity and constant development as a culture of recognition **of Achievements:** Feedback isn't just about areas that need improvement. Acknowledging achievements and successes is equally important in reinforcing positive behaviors.

5. **Professional Development Plans:** Use feedback as a basis for creating individualized professional development plans. This can involve training, mentorship, or opportunities for skill development.

6. **Feedback Tools:** Implement various tools and methods for feedback, such as performance reviews, 360-degree feedback systems, and regular check-ins to ensure that feedback is consistent and comprehensive.

7. **Actionable Feedback:** Feedback should be actionable, providing clear steps for improvement rather than just pointing out problems.

A strong feedback and improvement system supports employee growth, enhances team performance, and cultivates a corporate culture that values ongoing education and growth. It's a cornerstone for achieving individual and collective excellence.

Time off Policies

Time off policies outline the rules and regulations regarding the various types of leave or time off that employees are entitled to within an organization. These policies typically encompass several key aspects:

1. **Vacation Leave:** Defines the amount of paid time off granted to employees for leisure, rest, or personal reasons. It includes accrual rates, eligibility, and procedures for requesting and approving vacation time.

2. **Sick Leave:** Outlines the provision for paid time off due to illness or health-related issues. It includes the number of sick days available, documentation requirements, and conditions for using sick leave.

3. **Paid time Off (PTO):** Some organizations consolidate vacation, sick, and personal days into a single pool of paid time off, providing employees with flexibility to use the time as needed.

4. **Holidays:** Specifies the holidays recognized by the company and whether these days are paid or unpaid. It also covers rules for employees required to work on holidays and compensation policies for those hours.

5. **Bereavement Leave:** Covers the time off granted for employees due to the death of a family member or loved one. It outlines the duration, eligibility, and any documentation required.

6. **Maternity/Paternity Leave:** Details the time off provided to new parents for the birth or adoption of a child, including paid or unpaid leave, duration, and any associated benefits.

7. **Unpaid Leave:** Addresses instances where employees need extended time off that goes beyond the standard vacation or sick leave, allowing for personal or family-related reasons.

8. **Procedures for Requesting Time Off:** Details the process for requesting time off, such as advance notice requirements, the use of an online system, or specific forms to fill out.

These policies are designed to ensure fairness, compliance with legal requirements, and consistency in the way time off is managed within the organization. Clear and well-communicated time off policies contribute to employee satisfaction and work-life balance.

Training on Stress Management:

Training on stress management equips individuals with the knowledge, skills, and techniques to recognize, cope with, and mitigate stress in both personal and professional life. Here's how it typically works:

1. **Understanding Stress:** The training begins by explaining the concept of stress, its causes, and its effects on mental, emotional, and physical health. This helps participants identify their stress triggers and understand the importance of managing stress.

2. **Recognizing Symptoms:** Participants learn to identify stress's telltale signs and effects in both themselves and other people. This might include changes in behavior, mood, productivity, or physical symptoms like headaches or fatigue.

3. **Coping Strategies:** The training introduces various coping mechanisms such as relaxation techniques, mindfulness, time management, and problem-solving skills. These strategies help individuals manage stress more effectively.

4. **Resilience Building:** Training often focuses on developing resilience, which entails learning how to recover from stressful situations. This might include fostering positive thinking, enhancing problem-solving skills, and building a support network.

5. **Work-Life Balance:** Understanding the importance of maintaining a healthy work-life balance and providing

strategies to achieve It is an essential part of training in stress management.

6. **Support Systems:** Encouraging participants to seek support and communicate effectively with colleagues and managers when feeling overwhelmed. This can involve creating a supportive workplace culture.

7. **Continual Improvement:** Stress management training isn't a one-time event. It should be ongoing, with periodic check-ins, refresher courses, and opportunities for individuals to share what works best for them.

Training on stress management aims to not only mitigate stress but also to foster a more resilient and mentally healthy workforce. It empowers individuals to handle stress more effectively, leading to improved well-being and productivity.

Encourage Physical Activity:

In today's remote work landscape, staying physically active can often take a backseat. Encouraging a physically active lifestyle within a remote team is crucial for maintaining both the health and productivity of team members. To promote this, several strategies can be employed:

1. **Virtual Gym Access:** Provide subscriptions or discounts to online fitness platforms or local gyms. It could include

virtual classes, workout routines, or access to fitness apps that team members can use to exercise at their convenience.

2. **Fitness Challenges:** Organize team-wide fitness challenges, such as step count competitions, workout routines, or even yoga sessions. It fosters a sense of camaraderie while encouraging everyone to engage in physical activities.

3. **Scheduled Movement Breaks:** Encourage short, regular breaks throughout the workday for movement. Implementing stretch breaks, short walks, or group exercises via video calls can revitalize energy and focus.

4. **Supportive Environment:** Create a culture that values and supports physical activity. Encourage discussions about health, share success stories, and provide resources and tips for staying active.

5. **Personalized Support:** Offer guidance from fitness experts, nutritionists, or health professionals through workshops, webinars, or one-on-one sessions. Tailoring advice to individual team members' needs can greatly enhance their motivation to stay active.

By incorporating these strategies into the team's remote work environment, you can significantly contribute to the overall well-being and productivity of team members. An active lifestyle not only improves physical health but also positively impacts mental well-being, leading to a more engaged and motivated team.

Crisis Support:

Crisis support involves creating structured procedures to aid employees during challenging times, be it personal hardships or organizational crises. Here's how it can be implemented:

1. **Counseling Services:** Provide access to professional counselors or therapists who can offer guidance and support. It can be through an employee assistance program (EAP), which allows employees to seek confidential counseling and advice.

2. **Clear Communication Channels:** Establish clear lines of communication for employees to express concerns or seek help. This might include a designated point of contact, whether within HR or through a specific crisis response team.

3. **Training and Resources:** Offer training to managers and team leaders on how to recognize and handle crises. Additionally, provide resources such as toolkits or guidelines on how employees can access support in times of need.

4. **Flexibility and Supportive Policies:** Implement flexible work policies that accommodate employees facing personal or family crises. This might include flexible hours, extended leave, or remote work options.

5. **Organizational Response Plan:** Create a structured plan to address crises affecting the organization. This might involve clear steps for communication, resource allocation, and support systems to ensure employees feel secure and informed.

The goal is to create a supportive environment that acknowledges and actively assists employees during challenging situations, ensuring their well-being and readiness to face personal or organizational crises.

Clear Expectations:

Establishing clear expectations in the workplace is vital for minimizing ambiguity and stress. Here's how it can be achieved:

1. **Detailed Job Descriptions:** Ensure that job roles are well-defined and communicated effectively. This includes outlining responsibilities, goals, and performance expectations for each role within the organization.

2. **Regular Communication:** Foster an environment where open communication is encouraged. This involves regular check-ins between managers and their team members to discuss expectations, progress, and any changes in responsibilities.

3. **Setting SMART Goals:** Encourage the setting of Specific, Measurable, Achievable, Relevant, and Time-bound (SMART) goals. This aids in creating a clear roadmap for employees, ensuring they understand what is expected and how their performance will be evaluated.

4. **Feedback Mechanisms:** Establish a feedback system that provides constructive input on performance. This helps employees understand how well they are satisfying standards and areas in need of development.

5. **Adaptability and Flexibility:** Acknowledge that roles and expectations may evolve. Communicate these changes clearly and ensure employees have the necessary support to adapt.

By providing clear, well-defined expectations, employees gain a sense of direction and purpose in their roles, which significantly reduces stress and uncertainty. This clarity allows them to focus on their tasks and perform more effectively.

Recognition Programs:

Recognition programs are structured initiatives designed to acknowledge and reward employees for their exceptional contributions, achievements, or exemplary behavior. Here's how they typically work:

1. **Defined Criteria:** These programs usually have clearly defined criteria outlining what constitutes outstanding performance or behavior. This could include meeting specific goals, demonstrating leadership qualities innovative ideas, or going above and beyond their role.

2. **Variety of Recognition:** Recognition can take various forms, such as verbal praise, certificates, awards, public acknowledgment in team meetings, or inclusion in a 'Wall of Fame.' It can also involve monetary rewards, bonuses, or additional benefits.

3. **Consistency and Fairness:** these programs should be consistent and transparent. Employees should understand the criteria for recognition and how the selection process works.

4. **Regular and Timely Recognition:** Recognition should be timely, happening as soon as possible after the exemplary performance or achievement. Regular acknowledgment

keeps the motivation high and fosters a culture of appreciation.

5. **Involvement of Peers and Managers:** Peer-to-peer recognition can be as impactful as manager-led recognition. Creating a system where colleagues can nominate or commend each other can be very powerful.

These programs play a significant role in boosting employee morale, motivation, and engagement. They help create a positive work culture where employees feel valued, appreciated, Certainly, here are a few additional aspects of effective recognition programs:

1. **Customization:** Tailoring recognition to individual preferences can make it more meaningful. Some employees might prefer public acknowledgment, while others might appreciate a private thank-you note.

2. **Long-Term Impact:** Recognition programs should have a lasting impact beyond immediate rewards. They should contribute to the employee's sense of belonging, job satisfaction, and loyalty to the organization.

3. **Alignment with Company Values:** Recognition programs should reinforce the values and goals of the organization. This ensures that recognized behavior aligns with the company's overall objectives.

4. **Feedback Loop:** Encourage feedback from employees about the recognition programs. This helps in understanding what forms of recognition are most meaningful and how the programs can be improved.

5. **Celebration Events:** Special events or ceremonies dedicated to honoring successes may be a potent method to acknowledge outstanding work. This could include an annual awards ceremony or dedicated appreciation days.

When designed and executed thoughtfully, recognition programs can be a key driver in cultivating a culture of gratitude and excellence, as well as creating a good work atmosphere.

Peer Support Networks:

Peer support networks within embedded remote teams involve fostering an environment where team members can connect, share experiences, and provide mutual assistance. Here's how this can be implemented:

1. **Communication Platforms:** Utilize collaboration tools, forums, or dedicated channels where team members can openly discuss challenges, share experiences, and seek advice. This could be within existing communication tools or specific platforms for such discussions.

2. **Encouraging Participation:** Actively encourage team members to participate in these networks. Highlight the benefits of sharing experiences and seeking support from peers, emphasizing that it's a safe and supportive environment.

3. **Mentorship and Guidance:** Encourage more experienced team members to act as mentors or guides for newer or less experienced colleagues. This fosters a culture of learning and support within the team.

4. **Diverse Perspectives:** Emphasize the importance of diverse perspectives. Encourage team members from different backgrounds, roles, or experiences to contribute, allowing for a broader range of insights and solutions.

5. **Structured Support Programs:** Implement structured programs such as buddy systems or mentorship pairings. This can help new employees integrate more smoothly into the team and provide ongoing support.

6. **Recognition and Appreciation:** Acknowledge and celebrate the contributions and assistance provided within these peer support networks. This encourages continued engagement and fosters a culture of appreciation.

By encouraging the development of peer support networks, remote teams can benefit from shared knowledge, enhanced problem-solving, and increased camaraderie. It strengthens the team's resilience and supports individual growth and development within the remote work environment.

Certainly, here are a few more facets of peer support networks within embedded remote teams:

1. **Training and Resources:** Offer resources or workshops on effective communication and supportive behaviors. This can help team members understand how to provide constructive support and feedback to one another.

2. **Team-Building Activities:** Organize virtual team-building activities or social events to strengthen the connections between team members.

3. **Moderation and Facilitation:** Consider having moderators or facilitators oversee discussions, ensuring they remain constructive and supportive. This can help guide conversations and maintain a positive atmosphere.

4. **Feedback Loops:** Implement feedback loops within the support networks. Encourage participants to provide feedback on the effectiveness of the network and any areas that need improvement.

5. **Promoting Psychological Safety:** Emphasize the importance of creating a mentally secure setting where team members feel comfortable sharing their experiences challenges, and seeking advice without fear of judgment.

Family-Friendly Policies:

Family-friendly policies are workplace strategies and benefits designed to support employees who have care giving responsibilities, particularly for their families. Here's how these policies can be implemented:

1. **Parental Leave:** Offer paid or unpaid leave specifically for new parents, allowing them time to bond with their newborn or newly adopted child. This can include maternity, paternity, and adoption leave.

2. **Flexible Scheduling:** Allow employees to adjust their work hours or work remotely to accommodate family needs. This can involve part-time work, job sharing, or compressed workweeks, enabling employees to balance work and caregiving duties.

3. **Childcare Support:** Provide or subsidize childcare services or offer on-site daycare facilities to help parents balance work and childcare responsibilities.

4. **Eldercare Support:** Implement policies that support employees who are caring for aging parents or family members. This can include flexible schedules, information on eldercare resources, or assistance programs.

5. **Support for Family Emergencies:** Establish policies that allow employees to take time off for family emergencies or unexpected caregiving needs without facing penalties.

6. **Lactation Support:** Create lactation rooms or spaces for nursing mothers to express breast milk comfortably upon their return to work.

7. **Education and Resources:** Provide resources, workshops, or access to information about balancing work and family life. This could include parenting classes, stress management workshops, or access to educational resources for parents.

Family-friendly policies aim to create a supportive and inclusive work environment, acknowledging and accommodating the diverse needs of employees with caregiving responsibilities. These policies not only support employee well-being but also contribute to higher job satisfaction, retention, and productivity.

Health Screenings:

Health screenings involve providing periodic check-ups or tests to employees, often on a voluntary basis, to detect and prevent potential health issues. Here's how they work:

1. **Regular Assessments:** These screenings are typically scheduled at regular intervals, focusing on various health

aspects like blood pressure, cholesterol levels, glucose levels, body mass index (BMI), vision, or hearing.

2. **Preventive Health Measures:** The screenings aim to detect potential health concerns early, enabling employees to take preventive measures or seek medical advice before any conditions escalate.

3. **Education and Awareness:** Alongside the screenings, these programs often include educational materials, workshops, or consultations with healthcare professionals. This helps employees understand their health status and learn about lifestyle changes or medical interventions that can improve their well-being.

4. **Confidentiality:** Emphasize the confidentiality of results to encourage employee participation. Confidentiality builds trust and reassures employees that their personal health information is kept private.

5. **Follow-up and Support:** Provide support and resources for employees who receive concerning results, including guidance on seeking further medical advice or assistance. Follow-up programs can offer ongoing support for health improvement.

6. **Customization:** Tailor the screenings to the specific health concerns or demographics of the employee population. For

example, focusing on issues more prevalent in a certain age group or occupation.

Health screenings are a proactive approach to employee well-being, promoting a culture of health consciousness and prevention within the workplace. By offering these services, employers not only invest in the health of their workforce but also potentially reduce healthcare costs and absenteeism by addressing health issues early on.

Community Involvement:

Community involvement in the workplace refers to engaging employees in activities or programs that contribute to and support the surrounding community. Here's how it works:

1. **Volunteer Programs:** These involve organizing events or opportunities for employees to volunteer their time, skills, or resources to support local causes, charitable organizations, or community projects.
2. **Corporate Social Responsibility (CSR):** Companies may establish programs to give back to the community, which could involve financial support, donations, or pro bono work for community development.
3. **Team-Building Activities:** Engaging in community projects can serve as team-building activities. Collaborating

outside of the typical work environment helps strengthen relationships among employees.

4. **Sense of Purpose:** Community involvement instills a sense of purpose beyond the workplace. Employees feel a deeper connection to the company as they contribute to causes they care about.

5. **Boost in Morale:** Participation in community activities often leads to increased job satisfaction and a sense of fulfillment among employees, fostering a positive work culture.

6. **Enhanced Public Image:** A company's involvement in community initiatives can boost its reputation and attractiveness to potential employees and customers.

7. **Skill Development:** Employees might acquire new skills or develop existing ones through volunteer work, which can be beneficial in their professional development.

By engaging in community involvement activities, companies not only contribute positively to their local area but also cultivate a sense of social responsibility and unity among their employees. This involvement can have far-reaching benefits, both within the workplace and in the broader community.

A comprehensive approach to employee well-being

A comprehensive approach to employee well-being encompasses a strategy that acknowledges and supports various facets of an employee's life, fostering a workplace that prioritizes their overall health and happiness. Here's how this approach works:

1. **Physical Health:** Supporting physical well-being through health screenings, fitness programs, access to wellness resources, and initiatives that encourage healthy habits, such as nutritious eating and regular exercise.

2. **Mental Health:** Providing resources and support for mental well-being, including stress management training, access to counseling services, workshops on resilience and coping mechanisms, and creating a stigma-free environment for discussing mental health.

3. **Work-Life Balance:** Encouraging flexible work schedules, remote work options, and policies that support a healthy equilibrium between work and personal life responsibilities. This helps reduce stress and burnout.

4. **Financial Wellness:** Offering support or guidance on financial planning, workshops on financial literacy, and access to resources that aid in managing financial stress.

5. **Career Development:** Providing opportunities for skill development, growth, and advancement through training, mentorship programs, or tuition reimbursement, fostering a sense of purpose and achievement.

6. **Social and Community Support:** Facilitating community involvement or social activities, encouraging team-building exercises, and creating an inclusive and supportive work environment that values diversity and belonging.

7. **Safety and Ergonomics:** Ensuring a safe and ergonomic work environment to prevent workplace injuries and promote physical well-being.

By addressing various aspects of their lives and creating a supportive workplace culture, companies can contribute significantly to their employees' overall health, satisfaction, and productivity. This approach often leads to increased employee engagement, retention, and a positive work environment.

Tips for Effective Leadership:

1. Clear Communication" in the context of leadership involves effectively conveying your vision and expectations to your team. Let's break down the components of this leadership principle:

- Articulating Your Vision: Clearly express the overarching goals, mission, and long-term objectives of the team or project. It aids in team members' comprehension of the goal and path, fostering a shared vision that aligns everyone toward a common goal.

- Expressing Expectations Clearly: Clearly communicate the specific duties, obligations, and performance standards for every team member when expectations are well-defined, team members clearly understand what is required, reducing ambiguity and potential misunderstandings.

- Fostering understanding: Ensure that your communication is accessible and understandable to all team members. Use language and terms that resonate with the team's diverse skill sets and backgrounds. Encourage questions and discussions to clarify any points of confusion.

- Alignment Among the Team: When your vision and expectations are clearly communicated, it promotes alignment among team members. Everyone understands their contributions and how they fit into the larger picture, enhancing collaboration and synergy.

In unleashing potential, clear communication plays a vital role by providing a roadmap for team members to realize their capabilities. When expectations are transparent, individuals can better channel their efforts and talents toward achieving the team's objectives, ultimately unlocking their full potential for personal and collective success.

2. Lead by Example" is a leadership principle that underscores the importance of a leader embodying the values and work ethic they wish to see in their team. Here's a breakdown of this concept:

- Demonstrate Values: As a leader, you set the tone for the team's culture. By consistently exhibiting the values you prioritize – such as integrity, accountability, or collaboration – you establish a standard that encourages others to follow suit.

- Work Ethic: Leaders who lead by example don't just articulate expectations; they actively demonstrate a strong work ethic. It involves being diligent, committed, and dedicated to your responsibilities. When team members witness your commitment, it motivates them to invest their energy and effort into their tasks.

- Consistency: Leading by example requires consistency in your behavior. Being reliable and predictable in your actions builds trust and credibility. This consistency helps create a stable and trustworthy work environment.

- Inspiration: Your actions can be a source of inspiration for your team. When they see you tackling challenges with a positive attitude or going above and beyond, it encourages a similar mindset in others. Your behavior becomes a model for excellence.

- Alignment with Expectations: Align your conduct with the expectations you have for your team. If, for example, you emphasize punctuality, make sure you're consistently punctual yourself. This alignment reinforces the importance of the stated values and expectations.

In essence, "Lead by Example" is about being a living representation of the principles and work ethic you want your team to embrace. It's a powerful way to create a positive and high-performing work culture by inspiring your team to adopt the same standards of behavior and commitment that you exhibit.

3. Empower Your Team" is a leadership approach that involves granting team members the authority and independence to make decisions and take ownership of their work. Here's a breakdown of this leadership principle:

- Encourage autonomy: Provide team members with the freedom to act autonomously in making decisions and completing tasks. This autonomy allows individuals to leverage their skills and creativity, fostering a sense of ownership over their responsibilities.

- Decision-Making Authority: Delegate decision-making authority to capable team members. Empowering them to make choices related to their tasks or projects not only expedites the decision-making process but also promotes a proactive and engaged mindset.

- Foster Ownership: When team members feel empowered, they develop a sense of ownership and responsibility for their work. This emotional investment often leads to increased dedication and a willingness to go above and beyond to ensure success.

- Trust and confidence: Demonstrating trust in your team members' abilities builds confidence and morale. When individuals know that their leader believes in their competence, they are more likely to step up to challenges and takes initiative.

- Skill Development: Empowerment is a tool for skill development. Allowing team members to take on new responsibilities and make decisions helps them acquire new skills, broadening their professional capabilities.

- Accountability: With empowerment comes accountability. Team members understand that they are responsible for the outcomes of their decisions. This accountability promotes a sense of pride and a commitment to delivering high-quality results.

- Adaptability: Empowered teams are often more adaptable to change. When individuals are accustomed to making decisions, they become more agile and responsive to evolving circumstances.

In summary, empowering your team involves creating an environment where individuals have the freedom to act, make decisions, and take ownership of their work. It enhances individual growth and contributes to a more dynamic and high-performing team.

4. Active Listening" is a communication skill that includes paying close attention to, comprehending, and reacting to a speaker. In a leadership context, this principle emphasizes attentively engaging with your team members to build trust and enhance understanding. Here's a breakdown of this concept:

- Pay Attention: Actively listening requires giving your full attention to the person speaking. Put aside distractions, maintain eye contact, and show that you are genuinely interested in what they have to say.

- Empathy: Demonstrate empathy by trying to understand the speaker's perspective. It involves hearing their words and grasping the emotions, concerns, or enthusiasm behind their message.

- Avoid Interrupting: Resist the urge to interrupt or interject your thoughts prematurely. Allow the speaker to express themselves fully before responding. It conveys respect for their opinions and encourages open communication.

- Reflective Responses: Provide responses that reflect your understanding of what was shared. It could involve summarizing key points, asking clarifying questions, or expressing empathy. Reflective responses show that you've actively processed the information.

- Non-Verbal Cues: Make use of non-verbal clues like smiling or nodding. To signal that you are engaged in the conversation. These cues contribute to a positive and supportive communication environment.

- Seek Clarification: If something is unclear, seek clarification rather than making assumptions. It demonstrates your commitment to truly understanding the speaker's message.

- Value Feedback: Actively listening to your team's concerns, ideas, and feedback communicates that their input is valued. In turn, fosters a culture of openness and collaboration.

- Builds Trust: Active listening is a key component in building trust within a team. When team members feel heard and understood, it improves the team's relationship with the leader, creating a more supportive and cohesive work environment.

In summary, active listening goes beyond hearing words; it involves a genuine effort to understand the more profound meaning behind the communication. This practice is crucial for effective leadership, as it builds trust, enhances communication, and fosters a positive team dynamic.

5. Adaptability" in leadership refers to the ability to be open to change and to adjust strategies when necessary. It acknowledges the dynamic nature of work environments and the importance of staying flexible. Here's a breakdown of this leadership principle:

- Openness to Change: Adaptable Leaders are receptive to new ideas, evolving circumstances, and changing conditions. They understand that the business landscape is dynamic, and they are willing to embrace change rather than resist it.

- Willingness to Adjust Strategies: Adaptability involves a readiness to modify plans and strategies when the situation demands it. This flexibility allows leaders to respond effectively to unforeseen challenges or opportunities that may arise.

- Proactive Learning: Adaptable leaders are proactive learners. They seek to understand emerging trends, technologies, and industry shifts. This continuous learning mindset positions them to make informed decisions in rapidly changing environments.

- Resilience: The capacity to overcome obstacles and navigate through uncertainties is a key aspect of adaptability. Resilient leaders maintain composure during challenging times, inspiring confidence and stability within their teams.

- Effective Problem-Solving: Adaptable leaders excel at problem-solving. They can assess a situation quickly, consider alternatives, and make decisions that align with the changing circumstances. This agility is valuable in addressing unexpected challenges.

- Team Collaboration: An adaptable leader fosters a culture of flexibility within the team. It encourages team members to embrace change, contribute ideas, and collaborate on finding innovative solutions.

- Strategic Thinking: Adaptability is closely tied to strategic thinking. Leaders need to anticipate potential changes and plan accordingly. This forward-looking approach positions the team to navigate transitions more smoothly.

- Customer-Centric Approach: In industries where customer preferences or market demands evolve rapidly, an adaptable leader ensures that the team remains customer-focused. It might involve adjusting products, services, or communication strategies to meet evolving needs.

In summary, adaptability is a critical leadership trait that enables leaders to navigate uncertainty and change effectively. It involves adjusting to current circumstances and anticipating and preparing for future shifts in the business landscape.

6. Recognition and Appreciation" in leadership involves acknowledging and celebrating the achievements of team members

to boost morale and motivation. Here's a breakdown of this leadership principle:

- Acknowledge Achievements: Leaders actively recognize and acknowledge the accomplishments of individuals and the team as a whole. This acknowledgment can be for reaching milestones, completing projects, or demonstrating exceptional effort.

- Timely Recognition: Providing timely recognition is crucial. Acknowledge achievements promptly to ensure that the connection between the effort exerted and the recognition given is clear. It enhances the impact of the acknowledgment.

- Personalized Recognition: Tailor your recognition efforts to individual preferences. Some team members may appreciate public acknowledgment, while others may prefer a more private form of appreciation. Knowing your team members and their preferences enhances the effectiveness of recognition.

- Celebrate Successes: Celebrate successes and milestones, whether big or small. This celebration can take various forms, such as team gatherings, shout-outs in meetings, or personalized notes of appreciation.

- Link to Values and Goals: Connect recognition to the values and goals of the team or organization. It reinforces the alignment of individual and team efforts with the overarching mission, fostering a sense of purpose.

- Motivational Impact: Recognition and appreciation serve as powerful motivators. When team members feel that their contributions are valued and acknowledged, it boosts morale, enhances job satisfaction, and encourages sustained high performance.

- Encourage a Positive Culture: A culture of recognition contributes to a positive work environment. It encourages a supportive atmosphere where team members feel appreciated and are more likely to support each other.

- Peer Recognition: Foster a culture of peer-to-peer recognition. Encourage team members to acknowledge and appreciate the efforts of their colleagues. It spreads positivity and strengthens team cohesion.

In summary, recognition and appreciation are essential components of effective leadership. Regular acknowledgment of achievements boosts morale and motivation and contributes to a positive and collaborative team culture.

7. Conflict Resolution" in leadership involves addressing conflicts promptly and diplomatically to promote a positive and collaborative work environment. Here's a breakdown of this leadership principle:

- Prompt Addressing of Conflicts: Effective conflict resolution requires dealing with issues as soon as they arise. Addressing conflicts prevents escalation and helps maintain a healthy team dynamic.

- Diplomacy and Tact: Leaders approach conflict resolution with diplomacy and Tact. It involves maintaining a calm and composed demeanor, using respectful language, and focusing on the issues at hand rather than personalizing conflicts.

- Active listening: Pay attention to the issues raised and the perspectives of all parties involved. Understanding each person's viewpoint is crucial for finding a resolution that addresses the root causes of the conflict.

- Neutral Mediation: Leaders often play the role of mediators. They should aim to remain neutral, avoiding taking sides. This neutrality builds trust among team members and ensures a fair and unbiased resolution process.

- Focus on Solutions: Encourage a solution-oriented mindset. Instead of dwelling on the problems, guide the team toward identifying constructive solutions that address the underlying issues causing the conflict.

Promote Open Communication: Establish a setting where team members may freely voice their worries. Misunderstandings are less likely to take place when there is open communication, and disagreements may be resolved before they get out of hand.

- Establish Clear Expectations: Set clear expectations for behavior and collaboration within the team. When everyone understands the expected standards, it reduces the potential for conflicts to arise.

- Follow-Up: After a resolution has been reached, follow up to ensure that the agreed-upon solutions are being implemented and that the conflict does not resurface. It demonstrates a commitment to maintaining a positive work environment.

- Provide Conflict Resolution Training:** Equip team members with conflict resolution skills. Training in communication, negotiation, and conflict management can empower individuals to handle disagreements effectively.

- Promote a Positive Culture:** Fostering a positive work culture where differences are respected, and conflicts are considered opportunities for growth contributes to long-term harmony within the team.

In summary, conflict resolution involves addressing conflicts proactively, employing diplomacy, and fostering a collaborative atmosphere. A leader's ability to navigate conflicts positively contributes significantly to a healthy and productive work environment.

8. "Providing growth Opportunities" in leadership involves actively supporting the professional development of team members

to help them grow both personally and in their careers. Here's a breakdown of this leadership principle:

- Identify Individual Goals: Understand the career aspirations and personal development goals of each team member. It involves conducting regular discussions to explore their ambitions and areas for growth.

- Tailor Development Plans: Create personalized development plans for team members based on their goals and areas of interest. These plans might include training programs, skill-building initiatives, and opportunities for hands-on experience.

- Training and Skill Enhancement: Provide access to training sessions, workshops, and resources that contribute to the acquisition of new skills or the enhancement of existing ones. It helps team members stay relevant and adaptable in their roles.

- Mentorship and Coaching: Facilitate mentorship and coaching relationships within the team. Pair less experienced team members with seasoned professionals to provide guidance, advice, and a platform for knowledge exchange.

- Promote a Culture of Continuous Learning: Encourage an ongoing learning environment where team members are encouraged to stay curious, explore new ideas, and seek opportunities for self-improvement. It could include supporting further education or certifications.

- Challenging Assignments: Provide challenging assignments that stretch the capabilities of team members. Assigning tasks slightly beyond their current skill level encourages growth and development.

- Feedback for Improvement: Offer constructive feedback aimed at helping team members improve. This feedback should be specific, actionable, and tied to their development goals.

- Recognition of Achievements: Acknowledge and celebrate the achievements and milestones reached by team members in their professional development. Recognition reinforces the value of their efforts and motivates further growth.

- Promotion Opportunities: Actively consider team members for promotion opportunities when they demonstrate readiness for increased responsibilities. It signals that growth and advancement are recognized and rewarded within the organization.

- Provide Resources: Ensure that team members have access to the necessary resources, both financial and informational, to pursue their professional development goals.

In summary, providing growth opportunities involves a proactive approach to nurturing the professional development of team members. By investing in their growth, leaders contribute to the overall success of the team while fostering a culture of continuous learning and improvement.

9. Decision-making skills" in leadership involve the ability to make well-informed and timely decisions, considering relevant input, especially from the team. Here's a breakdown of this leadership principle:

- Well-Informed Decisions: Leaders should gather and analyze relevant information before making decisions. It involves seeking data, insights, and perspectives to ensure a comprehensive understanding of the situation at hand.

- Consider Team Input: Effective leaders recognize the value of diverse perspectives. They involve their team in the decision-making process, especially when the decision impacts the team directly. This inclusion can lead to more well-rounded decisions and fosters a collaborative environment.

Timely Decision-Making: While it's important to gather sufficient information, leaders must also make decisions in a timely manner. Delayed decision-making can hinder progress and create uncertainty. Striking the right balance between thoroughness and timeliness is crucial.

- Risk Assessment: Decision-making involves assessing potential risks and benefits. Leaders should be adept at weighing the potential outcomes of different choices, considering both short-term and long-term implications.

- Adaptability: Effective decision-makers are adaptable. They can adjust their strategies and choices in response to changing circumstances. This flexibility is vital in dynamic and unpredictable environments.

- Clear Communication: After deciding, leaders should communicate it clearly to the team. Transparency helps team members understand the rationale behind decisions, promoting a sense of clarity and alignment.

Accountability: Leaders take accountability for their decisions. Whether the outcome is positive or negative, taking responsibility fosters trust and demonstrates leadership integrity.

- Decisiveness: Being decisive is a key aspect of decision-making skills. It involves the ability to make tough choices even in ambiguous or high-pressure situations. Decisiveness is often associated with confidence and leadership authority.

- Learning from decisions: Effective leaders see decisions, whether successful or not, as learning opportunities. They assess outcomes, identify lessons, and use this knowledge to inform future decision-making processes.

- Strategic Decision-Making: Leaders align decisions with the broader strategic goals of the organization. It ensures that individual choices contribute to the overall success and direction of the team or company.

In summary, decision-making skills involve a combination of analytical thinking, collaboration, and a strategic approach. Leaders who excel in this area can navigate complex situations, inspire confidence, and drive their teams toward success.

10. The capacity to appreciate people on a profound level" in initiative alludes to the capacity to comprehend and oversee both your feelings and the feelings of your colleagues, fully intent on encouraging an amicable work environment. Here is a breakdown of this initiative rule:

- Self-Awareness: Pioneers with the ability to understand people on a profound level are receptive to their feelings. They perceive how they feel and comprehend the effect of these feelings on their way of behaving and direction.

- Self-Regulation: This includes the capacity to actually oversee and get a handle on one's feelings. Pioneers with a high ability to understand anyone on a deeper level can stay created and pursue sane choices, even in testing or high-pressure circumstances.

- Empathy: Pioneers who can appreciate individuals on a profound level can comprehend and discuss the thoughts of others. It includes being sensitive to the feelings of colleagues, showing sympathy, and taking into account their points of view in navigation.

- Effective Communication: The capacity to appreciate individuals on a profound level improves relational abilities. Pioneers can communicate their feelings plainly and grasp the close-to-home signals of others, prompting more viable and sympathetic correspondence.

- Motivation: Pioneers with the ability to understand people at their core are, much of the time, self-propelled and can motivate others. They have a reasonable feeling of direction and can convey excitement, which adds to a good and roused group climate.

- Social Skills: Solid interactive abilities are a part of the capacity to understand individuals at their core. It includes exploring social circumstances successfully, building positive connections, and encouraging a cooperative and strong group culture.

- Conflict Resolution: Pioneers with the ability to understand people on a profound level succeed in settling clashes strategically. They comprehend the feelings engaged with clashes, stay fair-minded, and guide the group toward the goal in a productive way.

- Adaptability: Sincerely, smart pioneers are versatile despite change. They can explore vulnerabilities and assist their colleagues with adapting to change by understanding and tending to their feelings.

- Cultural Sensitivity: The ability to understand people at their core stretches out to perceiving and regarding social contrasts. Pioneers with this range of abilities value the different close-to-home articulations and correspondence styles inside a multicultural group.

- Building Trust: The ability to appreciate people on a deeper level adds to the structure of trust. At the point when colleagues feel comprehended and esteemed, trust is reinforced, making an establishment for an amicable and cooperative working environment.

In rundown, the capacity to understand people on a deeper level is an essential initiative expertise that adds to making a positive and amicable work environment. Pioneers who get it and deal with feelings really can explore complex relational elements, rouse their groups, and encourage a sound workplace.

"Continuous Learning" in leadership involves fostering a culture that encourages ongoing learning and improvement, both for the leader and the team. Here's a breakdown of this leadership principle:

- Personal Development: Leaders who value continuous learning prioritize their professional development. It involves seeking new knowledge, staying updated on industry trends, and refining leadership skills through self-directed learning, courses, or workshops.

- Modeling Behavior: Leaders set the tone for the team. By actively engaging in continuous learning, leaders model the importance of staying curious and adaptable. This behavior can inspire team members to embrace a similar mindset.

- Providing Learning Opportunities: Actively support and provide opportunities for the professional development of team members. It could include access to training programs, workshops, conferences, or mentorship initiatives.

- Skill Enhancement: Encourage the acquisition and enhancement of skills relevant to individual roles within the team. Leaders should identify skill gaps and work collaboratively with team members to address them through targeted learning opportunities.

- Knowledge Sharing: Facilitate a culture of knowledge sharing within the team. Encourage team members to share insights, best practices, and lessons learned. This collaborative approach contributes to collective learning and growth.

- Feedback for Improvement: Provide constructive feedback aimed at promoting continuous improvement. This feedback should be specific, actionable, and tied to both individual and team goals.

- Adapting to Change: Continuous learning fosters adaptability. Team members who are committed to learning are better capable of successfully adjusting to changes in the work environment, whether they are technological advancements or shifts in industry practices.

- Innovation: A culture of continuous learning supports innovation. Team members who are encouraged to explore new ideas and approaches contribute to a dynamic and innovative work environment.

- Performance Metrics: Establish performance metrics that reflect a commitment to continuous learning. Recognize and reward team members who actively engage in professional development and contribute to the learning culture.

- Reflection and Growth Mindset: Encourage a mindset of reflection and continuous improvement. Leaders and team members alike should view challenges as opportunities to learn and grow, promoting resilience and adaptability.

In summary, continuous learning is a dynamic and integral aspect of effective leadership. Leaders who prioritize learning contribute to a workplace culture that values growth, innovation, and the ongoing development of both individual team members and the team as a whole.

"12. Time Management" in leadership involves the effective prioritization of tasks and assisting the team in managing their time efficiently to maximize overall productivity. Here's a breakdown of this leadership principle:

- Task Prioritization: Leaders need to identify and prioritize tasks based on their urgency and importance. It involves distinguishing between tasks that require immediate attention and those that contribute to long-term goals.

- Setting Clear Goals: Clearly defined goals provide a framework for task prioritization. Leaders should work with the team to establish specific, measurable, and achievable goals, helping everyone understand the overall objectives.

- Effective Delegation: Delegating tasks according to team members' strengths and capabilities is a crucial aspect of time management. Leaders should empower team members to take ownership of specific responsibilities.

- Time Blocking: Encourage the use of time-blocking techniques, where specific blocks of time are allocated to focus on particular tasks or projects. It helps minimize distractions and enhances concentration.

- Utilizing technology: Leaders can introduce or recommend tools and technologies that aid in time management, such as project management software, communication platforms, and scheduling applications.

- Regular Check-Ins: Schedule regular check-ins to assess progress on tasks and projects. It allows leaders to provide guidance, identify potential roadblocks, and make adjustments to prioritize if needed.

- Setting Realistic Deadlines: Establish realistic deadlines for tasks, considering the complexity of the work and the resources available. Unrealistic timelines can lead to stress and decreased overall productivity.

- Encouraging Breaks: recognize the importance of breaks for maintaining focus and productivity. Encourage short breaks to recharge and avoid burnout, as sustained periods of intense work can be counterproductive.

- **Time Management Training:** Provide training or resources on effective time management techniques for the team. It can include workshops, seminars, or access to relevant literature on optimizing work processes.

- **Flexibility and Adaptability:** Recognize that unexpected challenges and changes may occur. Leaders should guide the team in remaining flexible and adaptable to ensure effective time management in dynamic environments.

In summary, effective time management in leadership involves a combination of strategic planning, effective delegation, technology utilization, and a commitment to ongoing improvement. By optimizing time usage, leaders contribute to a more productive and efficient work environment for the entire team.

Promote Collaboration" in leadership involves creating an environment that encourages team members to share ideas, work together on projects, and leverage each other's strengths. Here's a breakdown of this leadership principle:

Encourage open communication to foster an atmosphere where team members are at ease with open communication expressing their ideas, opinions, and concerns. This open dialogue fosters a foundation for collaboration.

- **Encouraging idea Sharing:** Actively encourage team members to share their ideas and insights. It can be done through regular team meetings, brainstorming sessions, or dedicated platforms for idea exchange.

- **Team Building Activities:** Organize team-building activities that promote interaction and strengthen relationships among team members. It could include workshops, off-site events, or collaborative projects.

- **Recognizing Diverse Strengths:** Acknowledge and appreciate the diverse abilities and strengths that every team member contributes. Understanding and leveraging these strengths contributes to a more effective and well-rounded team.

- **Cross-Functional Collaboration:** Encourage collaboration across different departments or functional areas. This cross-functional collaboration can lead to innovative solutions and a more comprehensive approach to projects.

- Providing Collaborative Tools: Equip the team with the necessary tools and technologies to facilitate collaboration. It could include project management software, communication platforms, and file-sharing systems.

- **Facilitating Team Workshops:** Conduct workshops or training sessions focused on enhancing collaboration skills. It could involve team-building exercises, communication training, or workshops on effective collaboration techniques.

- **Setting Clear Goals:** Clearly define team goals and objectives. When everyone understands the collective mission, It fosters cooperation and a feeling of purpose among participants toward common objectives.

Recognition of Collaborative Efforts: Recognize and celebrate instances of successful collaboration. This acknowledgment reinforces the value of teamwork and encourages continued collaboration among team members.

- **Lead by Example:** Demonstrate a collaborative mindset through your actions. Leaders who actively participate in collaborative efforts set a precedent for the team, reinforcing the importance of working together.

In summary, promoting collaboration involves creating a supportive environment where team members feel empowered to collaborate, share ideas, and contribute to collective success. Leaders play a vital part in encouraging this cooperative culture by setting expectations, providing resources, and leading by example.

"13. Encourage Risk-Taking" in leadership involves fostering a culture where calculated risks are welcomed, enabling team members to step outside their comfort zones and innovate. Here's a breakdown of this leadership principle:

- Define a Safe Environment: Clarify that the team operates in a safe and supportive environment where taking calculated risks is encouraged. Team members should feel secure in expressing new ideas and exploring innovative approaches.

- Clarify the Difference between Calculated and Reckless Risks: emphasize the importance of calculated risks – those based on thorough analysis and understanding of potential outcomes. Distinguish between thoughtful, strategic risk-taking and impulsive or reckless behavior.

- Learning from Failure: Instill a mindset that sees failure as a chance for growth and development rather than a negative outcome. Encourage team members to analyze failures, extract lessons, and apply these insights to future endeavors.

- Provide Resources and Support: offer the necessary resources and support for team members to explore new ideas. It might include training, mentorship, or access to tools and technologies that facilitate innovation.

- Celebrate Innovation: Recognize and celebrate instances of successful risk-taking and innovation. This acknowledgment reinforces the value of creativity and encourages a culture where individuals are willing to push boundaries.

- Promote Entrepreneurship: Encourage entrepreneurial activities within the team – initiatives that operate like entrepreneurial ventures within the confines of the organization. It allows team members to explore and develop new ideas with a degree of autonomy.

- Establish a Feedback Loop: Create a feedback mechanism that allows team members to share insights, challenges, and outcomes of their risk-taking endeavors. This feedback loop promotes continuous improvement and informs future decision-making.

- Set an Example: Leaders should lead by example, demonstrating a willingness to take calculated risks themselves. When team members see their leaders embracing innovation, they are more likely to follow suit.

- Balance and Alignment: Help team members strike a balance between risk and alignment with organizational goals. Ensure that innovative efforts align with the broader mission and vision while encouraging creative thinking.

- Promote an environment where team members are always improving and constantly looking for better methods to accomplish objectives. This mindset supports ongoing innovation and the exploration of new possibilities.

In summary, encouraging risk-taking involves creating an environment that values innovation, learning from experimentation, and strategically pushing boundaries. Leaders play a pivotal role in shaping this culture by providing support, celebrating successes, and fostering a mindset that views calculated risks as essential for growth and progress.

"Inspire a Growth Mindset" in leadership involves cultivating a culture within the team that emphasizes the conviction that aptitudes may be enhanced by commitment and diligence. Here's a breakdown of this leadership principle:

- The conviction that aptitudes may be enhanced by commitment and diligence. It involves encouraging curiosity, providing opportunities for skill development, and promoting a positive attitude toward challenges.

- Model a Growth Mindset: Leaders should exemplify a growth mindset by embracing challenges, persisting through setbacks, and actively seeking opportunities for learning and development. Modeling this mindset sets a powerful example for the team.

- Encourage Effort and Persistence: emphasize the importance of effort and persistence over innate talent. Encourage team members to see challenges as opportunities for growth rather than as indicators of limitations.

- Acknowledge and Celebrate progress: Recognize and celebrate individual and team progress. Acknowledging incremental improvements reinforces the idea that growth is a continuous process and should be appreciated at every stage.

- Provide Constructive Feedback: Offer feedback that is constructive and focused on areas for improvement. Frame feedback in a way that encourages team members to see it as valuable input for growth rather than criticism.

- Promote Skill Development: Encourage team members to actively seek opportunities for skill development. It might involve training programs, workshops, or mentorship initiatives aimed at expanding their professional capabilities.

- Normalize Setbacks as Learning Opportunities:** Reinforce the idea that setbacks are a natural part of the learning process. Help the team view failures as opportunities to learn, adapt, and ultimately grow stronger.

- Create a Culture of Collaboration: A growth mindset is often fostered in collaborative environments. Encourage teamwork, knowledge-sharing, and mentorship to facilitate a culture where team members support each other's development.

- Set Stretch Goals: Encourage the team to set stretch goals that challenge their current abilities. These goals should be ambitious yet achievable with effort and dedication, promoting a mindset of continuous improvement.

- Provide Learning Resources: Equip the team with resources that support ongoing learning. It could include access to educational materials, workshops, or platforms that facilitate skill-building and professional development.

In summary, inspiring a growth mindset involves creating a culture that values learning, effort, and resilience. Leaders play a pivotal role in shaping this mindset by modeling the desired behavior, providing support, and reinforcing the belief that individuals and teams can continually develop and improve.

The ROI of Embedded Remote Teams

In the final chapter, we explore the tangible returns on investment (ROI) that organizations can realize by embracing embedded remote teams. From financial gains to enhanced productivity and employee satisfaction, we'll examine the measurable impact of remote work strategies.

1. *Measuring Success and Performance Metrics*

Dive into key performance indicators (KPIs) and metrics that organizations can use to measure the success of embedded remote teams. It includes productivity metrics, project completion rates, and employee satisfaction surveys.

2. *Quantifying the Impact on Employee Satisfaction*

Explore the direct correlation between remote work and employee satisfaction. Understand how flexible work arrangements contribute to higher job satisfaction, leading to increased retention rates and a positive company culture.

3. *Demonstrating Financial Savings*

Delve into the financial benefits of adopting embedded remote teams. Analyze cost savings related to reduced office space, utilities, and other overhead expenses, showcasing the positive impact on the organization's bottom line.

4. *Increased Productivity and Efficiency*

Examine how remote work can lead to increased productivity and efficiency. Explore case studies and data illustrating the benefits of fewer workplace distractions, minimized commute times, and the ability to tailor work environments for optimal focus.

By understanding and quantifying the ROI of embedded remote teams, organizations can make informed decisions, justify their remote work strategies, and further optimize their approach to ensure sustained success in the evolving landscape of the modern workplace.

CONCLUSION

"Unleashing Potential: The Power and Benefits of Embedded Remote Teams" has explored the transformative journey of remote work from a mere necessity to a strategic advantage for organizations. We've navigated through the advantages, challenges, and success stories, delving into the tools, leadership principles, and measures to ensure the well-being of embedded remote teams.

As we stand at the crossroads of the future of work, it is evident that embedded remote teams are not just a response to external factors but a proactive approach to harnessing the full potential of a globalized, digital workforce. Organizations that embrace this shift stand to gain not only financial savings but also enhanced productivity, a diverse talent pool, and increased employee satisfaction.

The lessons learned from successful case studies, coupled with the practical tips and strategies outlined in this e-book, serve as a guide for organizations aspiring to not only adapt but thrive in the dynamic landscape of remote work. By fostering clear communication, embracing technology, prioritizing employee well-being, and measuring the ROI of remote teams, organizations can chart a course toward sustained success and innovation.

As we bid farewell to traditional work models, let "Unleashing Potential" be a catalyst for positive change, inspiring organizations to embrace embedded remote teams and unlock unprecedented opportunities in the ever-evolving world of work.